PRAISE FOR JOHN "T[...]
AND *AN ACCIDENTAL [...]*

"John 'The Penguin' Bingham has touched a nerve with runners worldwide like no one in the last decade. He's funny but serious, informal but inspirational, and his spoken and written words have become the rallying cry for tens of thousands of runners who have found a patron saint where they least expected one—in the back of the pack. With The Penguin as their leader, they have found not just the courage to start, but also the determination to finish."

—*Amby Burfoot*, Runner's World *magazine*

"John 'The Penguin' Bingham does it again! *An Accidental Athlete* is a charming, witty, and relatable tale of John finding himself through running. In this great book he shares his journey with us one stride and two laughs at a time."

—*Deena Kastor, American marathon record holder, Olympic medalist, and 12-time national champion*

"Most of us can truly identify with John Bingham's story: There are no gold medals, no laurel wreaths, no world records. But John shows us that we have something more important: a chance, if we have the will and believe in ourselves. Because of runners like John, the wall of intimidation has crumbled, and tens of thousands of Americans are now believing in themselves. John has helped raise self-esteem and self-confidence in people all over the world. Nothing is more important to a person's well-being."

—*Dave McGillivray, Boston Marathon race director*

"John Bingham is Edward Abbey, Frank Shorter, Brad Pitt and George Carlin all wrapped in one. John as writer has a lesson or tale in all his adventures. I learn so much about myself

reading *The Penguin Chronicles*. As a speaker he is funny, sincere and lovable."
                                                                            —*Bart Yasso*, Runner's World *magazine*

"*An Accidental Athlete* is a great read and an affirmation of why we run. The next time you find yourself in doubt, bring The Penguin with you and you'll be glad you did."
                                   —*Kathrine Switzer, first woman to officially run the Boston Marathon,*
                                            New York City Marathon winner, and author of Marathon Woman

"*An Accidental Athlete* is a book for everyone. Current exercisers will smile, as the mistakes John made are ones we have all made. Nonexercisers will see that—like Oprah— anyone can become an 'adult-onset athlete.' Get on the Penguin bus because it is leaving the station!"
                                                —*Running Doc™, Lewis G. Maharam, MD,*
                                          author of Running Doc's Guide to Healthy Running

"When John steps in front of an audience, the quiet-spoken college prof disappears, and he becomes The Penguin. Behind his humor lies an invitation to everyone, of any size and speed, to fit as comfortably into this sport as he did at his start."   —*Joe Henderson, former editor of* Runner's World *magazine*

"John Bingham is the voice of the millions of those who are beginning to exercise each year. John feels their concerns and, with humor, provides the motivation to keep going."
                          —*Jeff Galloway, running coach and author of* Marathon: You Can Do It!

"John Bingham brings a bit of irreverence and a big dose of humor to his talks about running and races. He gets you to laugh, and we need that before races!"
                                                  —*Bill Rodgers, 4-time winner of the*
                                          Boston Marathon and New York City Marathon

An ACCIDENTAL ATHLETE

An ACCIDENTAL ATHLETE

A Funny Thing Happened on the Way to Middle Age

JOHN "The Penguin" BINGHAM

BOULDER, COLORADO

3002 Sterling Circle, Suite 100
Boulder, Colorado 80301 USA
(303) 440-0601 · Fax (303) 444-6788
E-mail velopress@competitorgroup.com

Distributed in the United States and Canada by Ingram Publisher Services

Library of Congress Cataloging-in-Publication Data
Bingham, John, 1948–
An accidental athlete: a funny thing happened on the way to middle age /
John "The Penguin" Bingham.
p. cm.
ISBN 978-1-934030-73-8 (pbk.)
1. Bingham, John, 1948– 2. Runners (Sports)—United States—Biography.
3. Running—Anecdotes. I. Title.
GV1061.15.B56A3 2011
796.42092—dc22
[B]
                                        2011012211

For information on purchasing VeloPress books,
please call (800) 811-4210 ext. 2169 or visit www.velopress.com.

This paper meets the requirements of ANSI/NISO
Z39.48-1992 (Permanence of Paper).

Cover design by Jason Farrell
Cover illustration by Jonathan Carlson
Interior design by Vicki Hopewell

Text set in Berling.

11 12 13 / 10 9 8 7 6 5 4 3 2 1

CONTENTS

CONTENTS

INTRODUCTION

I can't remember when I stopped wanting to play. As a young child all I thought about was playing. I played with toy trucks. I played baseball with my friends; I played basketball with my neighbors. I never worried about what I was playing, or even with whom I was playing. I especially didn't worry about how well I was playing.

At some point, though, I discovered that I wasn't very good at the very activities that brought me the most joy. This was a heartbreaking moment, and the discovery sentenced me to a long period of sedentary confinement.

What characterizes the act of play, it seems to me, is that it isn't defined by arbitrary performance standards. When I watch children play, when I remember what it was like for me to play as a child, I see only the joy in the activity itself, not the awful prospect of failure or even the promise of success. It's just play.

1

It's difficult for us as adults to give ourselves permission to enjoy something that we don't think we're very good at. We tell ourselves that once we've reached some level of proficiency, once we've acquired some minimum set of skills, then—and only then—will the activity begin to be fun.

At least that's the way it was for me.

I wanted to play tennis, but when after a few weeks I noticed that I wasn't getting much better at it, I quit. Even though I was having fun chasing balls around the court, I quit because I didn't think I was good enough to have fun.

For me, this dreadful thought that I had to be knowledgeable or skillful about something before I could enjoy it didn't stop with athletics. I used to enjoy drinking a glass of wine from time to time until I was told how much there is to know about wine before you can decide whether you like it or not.

I had tried to become a runner at a couple of earlier points in my life, and each time I failed because I ignored the most important aspect of my running experience: the pure fun of it.

I had the idea in my head that running needed to be, if not torturous, at least physically exhausting. For it to be good for me, for running to do me any good, for me to truly experience life as a runner, I had to be at the edge of fatigue and pain at all times.

This approach didn't work well for me.

No sane person is going to do something that repeatedly hurts him or her. People are not going to continue to hit themselves on the head with a hammer once it occurs to them that it hurts and that if they stop hitting themselves, the pain will go away.

Too often new runners—and walkers—take the attitude that they must continue to hit themselves in the head, that they must continue to accept that the activity they've taken up to make themselves feel better must first make them feel worse.

At least that's what I thought.

I thought that, as I've seen on a t-shirt, pain was weakness leaving the body. It turns out that the shirt is not correct. Pain is your body telling you that something's wrong and you should stop doing it. Pain is not your friend. Pain is not weakness. Pain is a symptom.

When I tried running in middle age, 100 pounds overweight, a 25-year pack-and-a-half-a-day smoker, drinker, and overeater, I had to take a different approach. I *knew* I wasn't going to be any good. So I just tried to enjoy myself.

And so it is that a funny thing happened on my way to middle age. I became an athlete. And not just any athlete but a runner—5K to marathon—a cyclist, a duathlete, a triathlete, and an adventure racer. All without taking a running step until I was 43 years old.

I forgot to mention that I am not just a merely mediocre athlete. I am awful. I am slow. Glacier slow. A slow runner, a slow cyclist, and a ridiculously slow swimmer. But I am having more fun than I have ever had.

---

*A funny thing happened on my way to middle age.
I became an athlete.*

For most of my life I was a musician. By the end of my career I was a pretty good musician. Not only was I a musician but all of my friends were musicians. I hardly knew anyone who wasn't a musician.

When I'd gather with friends, we'd do what musicians tend to do: eat, drink, and listen to music. We encountered the world as musicians. We didn't "hear" the world by choice; it was just the way we perceived our environment.

Later I was an academic: My friends were academics, and I lived in a world of academics. When I'd gather with those friends we'd do what academics tend to do: eat, drink, and complain about the students and the administrators.

We encountered the world with our minds. We thought about things a lot. We wondered about things but didn't do much else.

And so when I became an athlete—even an embarrassingly awful athlete—I suddenly found myself encountering the world as an athlete. I started to look forward to exerting myself. I started to like the feeling I got from the honest effort of trying to do just a little more than I thought I was capable of doing.

As the years passed I discovered that even if, despite my best efforts and intentions, I had almost no athletic gifts, I still enjoyed being an athlete. My enthusiasm and joy were a mystery to everyone around me. Surely I couldn't be satisfied. Surely I would become discouraged by my abject lack of talent. Surely I would quit.

Nope, I wouldn't. And nope, I didn't. What I know for a fact is that being an athlete, any kind of athlete, is a way of life that gives more back to you than you invest. When I run or walk or cycle, or do any of the hundreds of other activities I've tried, I get the gift of knowing myself. I get the gift of discovering the courage and tenacity and relentless inner strength that I possess.

As an athlete I've come to grasp the need to move my body. I understand that sitting behind a desk all day is not what my body is designed to do. I've learned to enjoy the simple movement of my body. I smile when I run or cycle or swim. I can skip again and jump again and walk as far as I want to without getting tired.

I have been released from a life of sedentary confinement.

See, it isn't what you do that makes you an athlete. It isn't how fast or how far you go. It's waking up every day knowing that you will take on whatever the world holds for you that day as an athlete. You will embrace the challenges—physical, emotional, and spiritual—because you know that as an athlete it's the challenges that make you stronger.

> **This book is an invitation for you to discover the accidental athlete in yourself.**

This book is an invitation for you to discover the accidental athlete in yourself. This is a description of one such journey of self-discovery, and in some ways it is a guidebook to use for your own journey.

There are no rights and wrongs in this book. There are no prescriptions, no rigid programs to follow, and no easy answers. This is a self-guided tour through one life, my life, and I hope that you will see yourself somewhere in my struggle to become an athlete.

My story is funny at times, sad at times, poignant at times, and just plain silly at times. I made some mistakes only once and others over and over again. You may have too.

In the end, though, I discovered that I didn't really make 100 mistakes, I made the same mistake 100 times. That mistake was believing that there was anyone else who could possibly know me better than I could know myself.

You are your best training partner, your best coach, your harshest critic, and your biggest fan. You are both the player and the cheerleader in your life. It shouldn't be any other way.

Join me as together we uncover the mysteries of the life of an accidental athlete.

PART I

The Kid Picked Last

ONE

SANDBOX NONNIE

I was a strange child. Not strange in a way that would make the neighbors nervous but strange in the sense that I was content with my own companionship. It wasn't that I didn't like other children; it was more that I was able to entertain myself by myself. That ability to define my happiness by my own standards turned out to be the beginning of a life of conflict with those who would seek to make me over in their image.

We had a sandbox in the backyard. It wasn't one of those fancy plastic sandboxes that kids have these days. It didn't have seats or pretty colors. It was made of two-by-fours nailed together in a square and filled with sand that my grandfather probably "borrowed" from some construction site.

That sandbox became the laboratory in which I experimented with much more than the Tonka toys with which I played. It was where I learned how to be social, how not to be social, how to share and how to hoard, and most importantly how to judge whether or not the other people in my sandbox were making my life happier.

A young neighbor couldn't pronounce my name, "Johnnie," so she called me "Nonnie." It was a nickname that my mother would use for the rest of my life. I was then, and still am in many ways, Sandbox Nonnie.

I learned early on that there were limits to playing alone. Being an island unto oneself may seem like a solid existential platform, but it doesn't make for much of a childhood. I came to understand that there were times when I would have to look outside my sandbox and include others in my plans and dreams.

Like nearly every young boy growing up in the 1950s, I wanted to be an athlete. Back then all of my heroes were athletes. Of course, in the 1950s in Chicago, the only sport we knew about was baseball, so my heroes were all baseball players. I wanted to be a baseball player.

There is still a hand-painted square on the back outside wall of my parents' house that was the strike zone of my youth. I would stand for hours just in front of my sandbox and throw a red rubber ball at that painted square. I didn't know for sure what a strike zone was, but I was sure that learning to throw the ball inside the square was a good thing,

When I look back, what amazes me most was how dedicated I was to my dream of becoming a baseball player. It wasn't as if I had even met any professional players. All I knew was what I saw on the old black-and-white television in the basement. Those grown men wearing funny pants were getting paid to do nothing more than play baseball.

Day after day, year after year, I threw that rubber ball against the brick wall. I had no way of knowing whether or not I was any good, and in fact that didn't matter to me. Not knowing whether I was any good wasn't what made throwing the ball fun. It was the act of throwing, pure and simple, that brought me joy.

I lived and played in a world of my own creation. Like A. A. Milne's Christopher Robin in the Hundred Acre Wood, I was surrounded by characters who represented all the qualities I wanted to have. I was brave, I was strong, I was cunning, I was respected. Eventually, though, I had to leave my backyard and my sandbox and join the other neighborhood kids in order to learn to play the game of baseball.

We weren't playing organized baseball. We were just a bunch of kids with bats and balls and gloves living out our fantasies. The kind of game we were able to play depended on how many of our friends we could get out of their houses.

If there were only two of us, we played catch. If there was a third person, we'd play "running the bases," where two kids would play catch while the third waited for someone to make a mistake and then would try to . . . well, run the bases.

If we could find a fourth kid, we could move to the field next to the elementary school and play "bounce or fly," where one person batted while the others played the field. There was some kind of scoring system whereby the fielders could earn enough points to become the batter.

We needed about eight people to have an actual game: a pitcher, a first baseman, and two guys playing a sort of hybrid infield/outfield position. Someone from the batting team would catch. With only four on a team we played "right field out," which meant that if the ball sailed into what would be considered right field, it was an automatic out.

It was on those scruffy baseball fields that I learned that sometimes, in order to get what you wanted, you had to be willing to adjust your attitude—and you definitely had to learn to share.

Whereas in the sandbox I could be cavalier about whether another child came to play, on the baseball field the ability and willingness to accept others with all their strengths and weaknesses were every bit as important as hitting and catching the ball.

"Chicago ball," or 16-inch softball, didn't require much in the way of equipment. We didn't use gloves, so all we really needed was a bat and a ball. The balls (still being used every summer) are as hard as rocks when new, and catching one on the fly was always an act of courage. All of us—*all of us*—at one time or another jammed a finger trying to make a catch.

> *Summer days began and ended with the dream of playing baseball.*

Over time, and especially if we let it sit outside in the rain, the ball came to have the consistency of pudding. When a ball got to that stage we could almost hook it with the bat and fling it, as in lacrosse. The secret to successful Chicago ball was keeping the ball in that sweet spot between rock-hard and pudding.

The result of this constant search for the perfect ball was that we would often encourage a player to join the game not so much for his physical gifts as because he happened to have the perfect ball. I learned early on that the best way to ensure my participation on a regular basis was to have a good ball.

Bats for 16-inch softball were not much more than rounded pieces of timber. Even so, there were bats of varying lengths, and players who could bring their own bats were highly sought after.

It was on that early field of dreams that I heard the expression "It's my bat and my ball, so I make the rules." It was also an early lesson in pragmatism. There were times when the game was more important than any particular play.

Twelve-inch baseball was a little more complicated and required a bit more equipment. We still didn't have to use gloves, but it was better if we did, and the bats had a bit more of a taper to them. As we got older and moved from 16-inch to 12-inch, the need to include less talented players with better bats and balls became more pronounced.

The ultimate goal for all of us aspiring young baseball greats was "hardball," the game played with the "league" ball—the ball they used in the majors. This was the Holy Grail for us. When someone turned up with a new "league" ball, our whole crowd of young boys would gather just to look at it as if it were made of gold.

To play hardball required complete cooperation among all the boys in the neighborhood. Everyone was invited to play because everyone brought what he had. It was magic. A game time was called, and from blocks away young boys gathered and laid their bats and balls at home plate for all to share.

Even our coveted and much-protected baseball gloves were common property. Anyone who had a glove left it out in the field when it was his team's turn to bat. That way those kids who didn't have gloves—for the most part because they couldn't afford them—would be able to play.

It was the perfect setting for learning the lesson of common goals and shared values.

I remind you that these were not games organized by adults. This was not T-ball. This was a bunch of neighborhood kids who recognized that in order for anyone to play, everyone had to play, not just the talented athletes. We needed everyone, from the smallest to the tallest, from the gifted to the clueless, in order to field a team.

Baseball wasn't just a game for us; it was a passion. We knew the names of the players, we chewed the bubble gum to get the baseball cards, and we memorized the stats. Baseball was life.

When I was 10 years old, several of my friends and I decided we would cut school and go to the Chicago Cubs' Opening Day. We lived just west of the city limits, and getting to Wrigley Field was no easy matter. The older brother of one of the guys figured out the bus schedule, and somehow we all managed to get to the game.

Of course we brought our gloves with us so that we could take home the ultimate souvenir: a game ball. In those days there was a net behind home plate, and we positioned ourselves behind the net where balls would sometimes drop over the edge. We spent the entire game there.

The games were televised locally, and unbeknownst to us, it turned out the camera from center field spent a fair amount of time focused on a ragtag group of young boys standing under the screen behind home plate. We were the stars of the day.

I learned about my stardom the hard way when I returned home and my grandfather, an avid baseball fan who never missed a televised game, asked me how school had gone that day. I said, "Fine." But unfortunately, he had seen us on TV and had been burning up for hours waiting for me to come home. His temper was legendary, and he let me have it. I don't think he was angry that we had cut school to go to a Cubs game. I think he was angry that I had lied. It was the last time I ever lied to him.

I spent nearly every summer during elementary school with a baseball glove hung over the handlebars of my bicycle. As often as not I was awakened by some friend, or group of friends, calling for me out in front of my house. In those days there were no air conditioners, so voices from outside carried clearly through the open windows and screen doors. Those summer days began and ended with the dream of playing baseball.

But it was also in those idyllic years that the haunting idea that I was not as good as the other boys began to take root. It wasn't that anyone ever said anything. It wasn't as if any of my friends would have called me out and told me I stunk. It was more subtle than that. They knew before I did that my skills were not up to theirs. I was the kid who always got to play right field. If you're not familiar with baseball, right-handed hitters, which included about 99 percent of the kids, rarely if ever hit a ball into right field. Thus, playing right field is like being sent to Outer Mongolia. You could go whole games without ever seeing a ball in that part of the outfield.

I was also the kid who batted deep in the batting order. The good hitters always batted first. The pitcher, assumed to be the worst batter on the team, batted ninth; I often batted eighth.

Looking back, I've come to understand what was going on. I couldn't be excluded; I had a bat, a ball, and a left-handed glove, after all. But I could be *sequestered*. I could be made to feel that I was permitted to be a part of the team but wasn't really considered an *essential* part of the team. I could play, but I would never be respected for my talent or skills.

My feelings of being a little bit less than everyone else just got worse as we grew older and moved to organized Little League play. Up to that point in my life I don't think there was a more devastating moment than when I went to the Little League tryouts and didn't make any of the teams. No one wanted me. No one.

I watched as all my friends from summer after summer of baseball were selected, and I was not. I knew that soon they would be wearing uniforms with numbers and cool baseball pants and even cooler baseball stockings, and I wouldn't. I wasn't good enough. It wasn't just a matter of opinion—it was a matter of fact.

I did play one season in the "minors" of Little League baseball. This was where all the uncoordinated, untalented boys went so that—I guess—they didn't feel completely left out. But we all knew we were the rejects, the outcasts. We didn't even have uniforms.

At 9 or 10 years old, I had already discovered that I wasn't athletic. Playing baseball was never fun again.

What I didn't know at the time, what my schoolyard friends didn't know, and what the Little League coaches certainly didn't know or recognize was that I was among the youngest boys in my class. I had started first grade when I was still 5 years old, and with a birthday in mid-December, I was younger than about 95 percent of my classmates. What this meant, I've learned, is that my physical development may have been age appropriate but was not on a level with that of my classmates because some of them would have been nearly a year older than I was. A year doesn't mean that much at age 60, but the difference in physical development between an 8-year-old and a 9-year-old is significant.

None of that mattered, though. Even if someone had told me that I wasn't as good as the other boys merely because of a fluke in the calendar, it wouldn't have helped. I wasn't as good as they were; I understood that much.

My best, I learned at that age, was not good enough. All those hours, days, weeks, and months of throwing a rubber ball against a brick wall were not enough. All the wishing, hoping, and dreaming were not enough. I was simply not as good.

That message of being "less than" was set in stone. As those elementary years went on it became more and more clear that I was not an athlete. What I had first learned on the baseball field was reinforced in gym class. With each passing grade the athletes began to bond with each other, and the nonathletes were left behind.

But dreams die hard, and in seventh grade I tried out for my school's basketball team. It would prove to be one of the more formative experiences of my young life.

TWO

DEATH BY DODGEBALL

I don't think that there can be a worse time to be a young boy than junior high school. By that age, just before their teens, the girls have discovered that their bodies are changing and that there is a world beyond themselves to explore.

Junior high boys, on the other hand, haven't even discovered the benefits of personal hygiene, which is why, in my experience as a student-teacher supervisor, every junior high school smells like boys who needed to change their underwear one day sooner than they did.

It's not that I was any different. I wasn't. By that age I had discovered cars and motorcycles and had begun a lifelong fascination with anything with an engine, but girls and hygiene were still a few years off.

There was a moment in seventh grade that so crystallized my experience with life, my body, and my skills and talents that telling it today, some 50 years later, still causes the hair on my arms to stand up. That moment was the first day of gym. The first day in the locker room. The first day that I would have to undress in front of complete strangers.

It's important to remember that in those days there was no such thing as a "social promotion." You either got promoted to the next grade because you learned what you were supposed to learn, or you were held back. There wasn't any particular stigma about being held back—it just happened.

For some of my school friends it didn't happen just once. It wasn't unheard-of for someone to take a couple of years to make it through a grade. This is by way of explaining how it was that there were boys in that locker room who ranged in age from the 11-year-olds like me to the 17- or 18-year-olds who had no intention of going to school beyond the eighth grade.

My neighborhood was a hardscrabble, blue-collar, working-class, and ethnically mixed area. My grandfather's formal education had ended at third grade. My grandmother made it through seventh grade. My mom and dad had graduated from high school, but it was not unusual for a young boy to join his father at the factory when he turned 18, no matter what grade he happened to be in.

So there I was, a very young 11-year-old who also happened to be the second-shortest boy in the seventh grade. By the way, it was a daily embarrassment to me, to the shortest boy, and to the early-blooming tall girls to have to line up *by height* to go to lunch.

That first gym class was so traumatic that I thought I'd never go to school again. Watching the other boys, some of whom had the early-warning signs of puberty and others of whom were in the full flower of adult manhood, change into their gym shorts was paralyzing. If there had been such a thing as home schooling in those days, I'm certain I would have begged my parents to let me stay home.

It wasn't just the physical differences in our bodies that bothered me; it was the general sense of not knowing how one progresses from the preteen to the semiadult physique. I simply couldn't imagine how the body I was looking down at could ever be like the bodies I was looking over at.

It was in junior high gym class that I was introduced to an activity left over from the Spanish Inquisition: dodgeball. I'm not sure who invented dodgeball, but I can almost guarantee you that it wasn't the shortest kid in the class.

The way we played dodgeball was that we chose sides, and half the kids in the class went into the middle while the other half formed a circle around them. The rules were simple: If the ball hit you, you were out. If you caught it, you stayed in. It was cruel by design.

> **I'm not sure who invented dodgeball,**
> **but I can almost guarantee you that it wasn't**
> **the shortest kid in the class.**

We played with a large red rubber ball. If this ball hit you in the face, it wouldn't injure you too badly, but it left a mark that wouldn't go away for days. If it hit you in the stomach, it took an hour or so afterward to catch your breath.

Every game was the same: The big boys would commandeer the ball and start making a verbal list of the kids who would be "taken out." The first ball was always aimed at one of the fat kids. I guess it was easy pickings, or maybe it was just their way of warming up.

The smaller, weaker kids never got to throw the ball. *Ever.* If somehow the ball did roll to one of us, we were immediately stripped of it. Only the big boys threw.

After the fat kids were gone, it was time to go after the kids with glasses. The teachers would remind us that we weren't supposed to aim at anyone's face, and especially not at the kids with glasses, as if somewhere in the big boys' demented, junior-high-male-hormone-addled minds was any room to pay attention to such admonitions.

Next it was time to take out the girls. Yes, the girls were spared until after the fat kids and the kids with glasses were out. I think it was because when there were nearly only girls left, the big boys could take better aim at them. These were the same girls whom a few years later they'd be trying to date—but some of the girls would never forget.

There was one advantage to being small. I could hide behind the fat kids until they were all gone. Then I could hide behind the kids with glasses. Then I could hide behind the girls. It wasn't unusual for me and some of the other small boys to be the last two or three people left in the circle.

The strategy at that point was to stand back-to-back like gladiators facing the lions. Paying no heed to common sense or the dangers of the situation, we would begin to taunt the big boys. This strategy only incensed them so that they threw the ball harder and harder.

We were merciless in our taunts. It was the only time when we, the younger and shorter, could hold any sway over the older and larger. In some way I suspect they admired our courage, if not our judgment.

Of course the game always ended the same way: One of the largest boys would throw that red rubber ball so hard that you knew catching it was impossible and that if it hit you straight up, you'd either lose an organ or be in a coma for months. So you stepped aside quickly and let it glance off you. And that was that.

As much as I hated dodgeball, standing there in the center, reflecting the stares of those bigger and stronger, was one of the most satisfying feelings I'd ever had. Years later, when others who were bigger, stronger, or more important stared me down, I remembered with considerable pride the courage of that young boy.

It wasn't just dodgeball that made junior high difficult for me. Unlike elementary school, where we had been under the care of one understanding classroom teacher, in junior high we had different teachers for different subjects. My undiagnosed dyslexia was becoming more of a problem, and my grades were dropping, I felt more and more isolated, and I was becoming a band geek. There's nothing wrong with being a band geek; it was just that I didn't *want* to be a band geek. I wanted to be an athlete. I didn't want to sit on the back riser and play trombone; I wanted to be out on the field playing baseball or in the gym playing basketball.

And so it was that at the beginning of my eighth grade year I pleaded with my parents to let me try out for the junior high basketball team. Get the picture in your head. I was still the second-shortest boy in the class. I was still one of the youngest boys in the class. I had already begun to establish myself as a white-buck-shoe-wearing band geek. But I wanted to be on the basketball team.

I think there must have been a minimum number of boys who had to be on the team in order to compete in the conference because somehow I made it onto the team. I made the *team*. I got a pair of real basketball shoes and a uniform that said "Rhodes" on the front and had a number on the back.

I was there for practice every day. I loved the drills. We passed the ball back and forth, we zigzagged across the floor, we got in line to shoot layups, and we practiced our free throws. After practice I'd stay and practice some more. I'd stand at the free-throw line and toss up ball after ball trying to make a basket. From time to time I did.

A neighbor had a basketball hoop in a backyard driveway. I spent hours dribbling on the concrete, shooting baskets, playing endless games of P-I-G and H-O-R-S-E by myself. I learned to shoot overhand like the big boys. I practiced until I couldn't practice anymore.

There was just one small problem with my being on the basketball team: I wasn't any good at playing basketball. Given the dual handicaps of size and age, no amount of practice would transform me into even a mediocre basketball player.

How did I know? I never got to play in the games. I was at practice every day. I worked harder than anyone else. I did my best, but, just as in Little League, my best wasn't good enough. The coach knew it. The other players knew it. Most importantly, I knew it.

I didn't quit, though. Just suiting up and going through the pregame warm-up drills was enough for me. I had made the *team*, and I was proud of it.

And then it happened.

We were playing our archrivals. It was a hard-fought game. The score went back and forth until, with a minute or so to play, we were just one point behind. The coach called a time-out. His plan was clear and brilliant: We would get the ball back, we would stall until there were just a few seconds remaining, and then we would make the basket and win by one point. Brilliant.

We players gathered around the coach to hear and fully absorb this winning strategy. Only one question remained: Who would be the one to take that final shot? Who on the team would be able to win the game?

To the amazement of the entire team, the coach said I would take the shot. Me. The kid who, until then, had not played one minute in any other game. The other team members shuddered in disbelief. Finally one of the older boys—he actually was about 17— asked the coach why in the world he would have me take the shot. His answer was simple: No one would be guarding me because no one would expect me to take the shot. Brilliant. Risky, but brilliant.

> **For many of us, the seeds of our later success can be found in our early failures.**

The team went out on the court, with me trailing behind. I knew without a doubt that this was my moment. My defining moment. I was being given a gift that I could never repay. I was going to be a hero. Like my athlete heroes, I was going to make the basket, score the points, and win the game.

The ball was tossed onto the court, and the plan began working exactly as the coach had drawn it up. The big boys were playing keep-away from the other team while I, completely ignored, slowly made my way to the position near the basket. The coach had been adamant: I was to go to *that* spot and wait for the pass. Once I had the ball in my hands, I was to set and shoot the basket.

With just seconds to go, the ball came to me. I had it in my hands. The moment had arrived. Rather than shooting overhand, however, I decided that I would be more accurate with a between-the-knees under-hand toss.

Up the ball went in a beautiful, sweeping arc. The rival players were glued to the floor, their eyes focused on the ball. My teammates froze in place, watching and waiting. Everyone in the gym was on their feet. The coach was jumping up and down. My moment was upon me.

Just as the buzzer sounded, the ball landed on the court. Not only had it not gone into the basket, it hadn't even gotten within feet of the basket. The crowd went wild. I stood there in utter disbelief. My moment had come, and I had blown it.

I'd like to tell you that the coach came up and put his arm around my shoulders and told me not to worry, that it had been his decision, that I had done all that was asked of me and had just missed the shot. But that isn't what happened. The coach was scream-ing, *"How could you miss that shot?"* at the top of his lungs; my teammates were walking by and yelling, *"You stink!"* Even the players on the other team joined in. I was humiliated.

Some small piece of me died that day on the basketball court. The young athlete in me didn't understand that moments like that come and go. The young athlete in me didn't understand that if I worked hard enough, another moment like that would come, and maybe *that* time I'd make the basket.

I don't remember the coach's name, and I couldn't tell you the name of even one other boy on that team, yet they were some of the most influential people in my life.

I never played organized basketball again. I have never been on another team. In many ways it was the end of a dream.

Back then I thought I must be the only person who had ever experienced that kind of failure and disappointment. Turns out it is a nearly universal experience.

As I've scratched the surface I've discovered that many of us, from successful athletes to musicians to academics and more, have had to overcome what seemed like a devastating breakdown when viewed through junior-high-school-aged eyes.

I also discovered that, for many of us, the seeds of our later success can be found in our early failures.

THREE

BOWLED OVER

As bad as junior high school was for me, high school was even worse. I entered high school at 13 years old. I was small. I was unathletic. I was a music geek. I was about as far from the cool teenaged boys in the 1960s-era movies as you could get.

If you've watched reruns of the *Happy Days* television show, you might think you know what it was like to be in high school in the early 1960s. You don't. High school was, for me at least, a kind of cosmic collision of worlds in which the me I so desperately wanted to be kept getting farther and farther from the me I was desperately trying to avoid becoming.

As in junior high school, there was a moment in high school during which it all became clear to me. In fact, it all became way *too* clear for me. That moment was the first day of swimming instruction as a part of the gym curriculum.

I have no idea why it seemed so important that everyone know how to swim that my high school dedicated two weeks to swim instruction every year. Of course I didn't understand why I had to learn to use a trampoline or parallel bars either. And wrestling—well, the rationale behind having to put my face next to the sweaty body parts of someone I didn't know and was pretty sure I didn't like remains a mystery to this day.

> *High school was a cosmic collision of worlds*
> *in which the me I so desperately wanted*
> *to be kept getting farther and farther from the me*
> *I was desperately trying to avoid becoming.*

Let me set the scene for my moment of enlightenment. One day we were told by our gym teachers (coaches of various sports who, it seems to me, were all returning war veterans suffering from undiagnosed post-traumatic stress disorder) that swim instruction would begin the following day. We were also told that we wouldn't need trunks because we'd be swimming in "whatever God gave ya."

That's right. Swim classes for high school boys were taken in the nude. Not in trunks. Not even in tiny Speedos. In the *nude*. And not just your freshman year but every year.

Remember that because there were no social promotions in those days, we had students in our junior high who were in their late teens. In our high school we had students who had left school for one reason or another and had then come back to finish and get their diplomas.

So, at 13, I found myself standing buck naked at the edge of the pool with other naked boys and men who ranged in age from 13 to 30. The first command was to get into the pool—which seemed like a blessing at the time—to "put your family jewels in the spit tray," and to kick like you meant it. I didn't dare turn around, but I can only imagine what the coach's view was of 200 bare-bottomed boys kicking like they meant it.

Think that was bad? Well, it just went downhill from there. We were taught all of the common strokes, including—you guessed it—the backstroke. There can be nothing more humiliating than having to swim naked, belly up, in a cold pool.

Not only did we have to learn swim techniques—in the nude—but we also had to learn lifesaving skills. That's right; we had to save a naked drowning victim by putting our arms around him and sidestroking to the edge of the pool. I shudder when I think of it.

If there was any saving grace to this annual humiliation, it was that as we less developed boys moved from freshman to senior, we were likely to find others for whom the magic of puberty was even more removed than it was from us. But that was hardly adequate compensation.

Gym class during the rest of the year was not quite as obviously embarrassing for the less-than-athletic among us, but the separation from the rest of us of those who were faster and stronger and could jump higher got ever more intense and more embedded.

The boys were separated by skill level after being tested. We were put through a variety of physical fitness tests that measured speed and strength, among other things. Based on these test results, we were grouped with boys of similar ability. The lowest level was the White Group—fat kids with glasses, mostly, including me. Boys with modest abilities were in the Red Group. Boys with better-than-average skills were in the Blue Group: the athletes.

At the top of the ladder was the Gold Group. These were the boys who had scored at the Blue Group level on every skill test. They were the anointed ones.

Five days a week, every week, we lined up with our skills cohort: the White Group, the Red Group, the

Blue Group, and the Gold Group. Whatever the activity was for that term, the boys in each set interacted only with others in their group. Whether it was baseball or basketball or gymnastics, the kids in the Blue and Gold Groups never had to spend time with the kids in the White Group. We were shunned as nonathletic an hour a day, five days a week.

But it wasn't only gym class that showed my lack of athletic skills at such an obvious level. I couldn't seem to resist putting myself in situations in which my abject absence of talent would be on public display.

In the area where I grew up, bowling was a very popular activity. I'm not sure we considered it a sport, exactly, but there were bowling alleys all over the place, and the Wednesday and Friday leagues were filled by the parents of my best friends.

Bowling was also a fairly inexpensive high school date night. Several couples could meet up at a local bowling alley, form teams, and spend hours together for nothing more than the cost of a few games.

This is by way of explaining how I found myself in the backseat of a friend's car with a girl whom I was desperate to impress, on my way to an evening of bowling. You see, I didn't know how to bowl. Worse yet, I had never even set foot in a bowling alley. I had seen bowling on television. I grasped the general concept but had absolutely no experience or skills.

My first inkling that I might be in over my head was when my friend pulled out his personalized bowling ball and shoes. His ball was a custom-drilled beauty that fit his hand perfectly. And his bowling shoes were elegant.

I was standing at the counter watching a man spray what I hoped was disinfectant into what appeared to be clown slippers and hand them to me and my date. We then had to find balls to use. This, it turns out, is the first and last skill test for new bowlers. Pick the wrong ball and the rest of the night is lost.

Being a typical high school boy on a date with a girl he was trying to impress, I of course picked up the heaviest ball I could carry. If my memory serves me right, the ball weighed about 80 pounds, give or take. It was solid black, and the finger holes were big enough for King Kong. My date grabbed a smaller, sparkly ball, and we made our way to the lane.

Everything was going great until it was my turn to bowl. As I approached the line, not having asked anyone for even the tiniest bit of instruction, I pulled the ball back as I had seen others do and promptly dropped it behind me. The laughter started immediately.

The laughter didn't stop when, on my second approach to the line, now with a death grip on the ball, I released it at the top of the swing, and it fell directly at my feet. It was over the line and not moving.

I reached down, grabbed it, and threw it down the lane with more or less of a hurling motion. The ball stayed in the wooden lane for almost 3 feet before falling ceremoniously into the gutter. That sight, along with the manager yelling at me that if I dropped the ball like that again and dented his wooden floor, I'd be thrown out, was enough to induce Coke-through-the-nose laughter from my friends and my date.

But I was undeterred. When the ball returned, I squared off with the pins, fully intending to send the ball rocketing toward them. With a Herculean effort, I pulled the ball back and—mindful of the manager's warning not to drop it—promptly hit the floor with my hand still stuck in the finger holes. I think my score that night was 6. It was also the end of my career as a bowler and the end of any chance of a second date with that girl.

It wasn't just bowling. Putt-putt golf was a disaster. Going to the batting cages was worse. Even the carnival games seemed beyond my athletic abilities.

Something had to change. I knew what I had to do.

That dream of being an athlete still burned strongly in my soul. I didn't care what it took. I didn't care how hard I had to work. I was going to get out of the White Group.

I spoke to the coaches and told them my goal. Their condescending smiles didn't deter me. I asked and asked and asked until they started to believe that I was serious. This small boy who hadn't even begun to shave was trying to convince them that he was going to be in the Gold Group someday.

It seemed hopeless at first. The standards for each group were printed in giant signs hung around the gym. You had to be able to run fast, leap far, jump high, throw accurately, and demonstrate that you were the consummate athlete. And you had to do it publicly.

By my sophomore year in high school I had worked my way up from White to Red. It might not have seemed like much to anyone else, but I was determined. I lifted weights. I practiced sprinting and jumping. I bothered the coaches all the time for more information.

By my junior year I was solidly in the Red Group. I had become, in fact, a leader in the Red Group. But I wanted more. I knew that the real athletes were still one group above me, and I was determined to be one of them.

As the testing began for my senior year, I was ready. I was in what at the time was the best shape of my life. I had lost weight. I was eating better and exercising more. I was beginning to live like an athlete even if I wasn't recognized as one.

The first few tests went well. I scored in the Blue on every one of them. The last test was the vertical jump. I don't remember the height we had to jump, but it seemed impossible to me. I was, after all, still short and small for my class. This final test would determine whether I would spend my senior year in a gold shirt or not.

We were given three tries. On my first attempt I missed, and missed badly. The coach administering the test shrugged as if to say, "Too bad." It made me mad.

On my second attempt I still missed, but not by as much. The coach was not enthusiastic, but he was at least paying attention. And I was madder still.

The third jump was an all-out, go-for-broke, noth-ing-to-lose effort. I felt my feet leave the floor. I reached up with my hand and slapped the wall as I felt myself reaching the apex of the jump. When I landed and looked up, I could barely believe it. I had done it. I had passed every test. I was going to get to wear a gold shirt.

> *Whatever my limitations were in terms of size or talent, they could be mitigated, if not eliminated, by hard work.*

Because I was now in the Gold Group, I got to line up with the other athletes. Suddenly I was in the company of the basketball players and the football players. I was playing baseball with the students on the school team.

But, truth be told, despite my having passed all the tests, I still wasn't really one of them. They were the "real" athletes, and I was not. What I learned, though, was that whatever my limitations were in terms of size or talent, they could at least be mitigated, if not eliminated, by hard work. Maybe the satisfactions that came from working hard would be private satisfactions.

I felt differently about myself after that. I had earned something that I could get only through my own efforts. Years later I would have that same feeling crossing a marathon finish line. But in that moment as a 16-year-old high school student, I was as close to being a real athlete as I had ever been.

FOUR

SMOKE AND PT

By the time I got to college, the dreams I had of being an athlete seemed to have been left far behind. I had become a musician—a trombone player—and all my time outside of school was taken up with practicing and rehearsals. I was in every musical ensemble that had trombones: marching band, concert band, orchestra, wind ensemble, jazz band, and trombone choir. Trying to be a better athlete was replaced by trying to be a better musician.

I had also discovered the joy of beer, and when I wasn't practicing or in rehearsal it wasn't unusual for me to be drinking.

What seems strange, looking back, is that in spite of the fact that I possessed some musical talent, it didn't mean that much to me to be considered a good musician. I did not hunger for it in the way I had hungered to be an athlete.

Stranger yet is the fact that the lessons I needed to learn to become an athlete—if not a great athlete, then the best athlete I could be—came not from a coach but from a conductor. His name was Roger Schueler.

Roger Schueler taught trumpet and conducted the Wind Ensemble at Millikin University in Decatur, Illinois. Although he was a classically trained conductor, Schueler's real love was jazz. And his real genius was in taking a group of mediocre young musicians and forming them into one of the finest collegiate jazz bands that ever existed.

> *I learned that to be a part of something great was better than being considered great.*

Roger Schueler was cut from the same philosophical cloth as Vince Lombardi. Lombardi has been quoted as saying that winning isn't everything; it is the *only* thing. For Roger Schueler, playing the music well wasn't everything; it was the only thing.

His rehearsals were more like an athletic practice than those of any other conductor I have ever worked with. We were there not to please and amuse ourselves but to give ourselves over to him first and to the music second.

There was no such thing as trying to do our best. We simply did our best. We did our best all day, every day. We showed up for every rehearsal ready to lay it on the line. We showed up ready to give him whatever he wanted that day.

His temper tantrums were legendary. If a musician played out of tune or committed the unforgivable sin of missing a note, Schueler could lay him open with surgical skill.

Being in that jazz band was the closest I had ever come to feeling that I was an important member of a team. I was a contributor, not a bench warmer, as I had been in junior high. It was in that rehearsal room that I learned what it meant to care more about the people around you than about yourself. I learned that to be a part of something great was better than being considered great.

Most importantly I learned that I wanted to be better than I was, not only for myself but to honor the efforts of the others around me. It was a lesson that I learned well even if I didn't fully understand it then.

After graduation I got *the* letter: I was going to be inducted. I had to go into the military. Even as I was taking the enlistment oath I couldn't figure out what was happening to me. But, as often happens, what seemed bad on the surface ended up being one of the best experiences of my life.

It turned out that for one glorious moment in my life, I got a glimpse into what it would be like to be an athlete. Even more importantly, I saw clearly that I *could* be an athlete. That time, oddly enough, was the 12 weeks during which I was going through the U.S. Army's basic infantry training. In contrast to the other times in my life, in basic I was one of the older trainees: a college graduate and someone who had enough life experience to be looked up to by the 18- and 19-year-olds who made up the rest of my training company.

In the weeks leading up to my enlistment date I started running. I had heard that you did a lot of running in basic training, and I wanted to get a head start on it. I bought a pair of gym shoes and started jogging around my neighborhood. I had already begun smoking in earnest and drinking more than I should, so the running didn't come naturally. It turned out, however, that it didn't matter. Nothing I could have done in the weeks leading up to basic training could have prepared me.

It was true that we ran a lot. We ran to meals. We ran to training sessions. We ran with packs. We ran with rifles. We ran and ran and ran.

The more I ran, the more I liked it. I would volunteer to be a road guard just so I could run ahead of the company formation and then run back into position. Unlike every other time in my life, I wasn't just pretending to be good at something—I actually was.

In fact, it turned out I was good at nearly every skill that was required in basic training. I was good at hand-to-hand combat. I was good at bayonet training. I was good with a rifle and with hand grenades. Instead of being one of the worst in the group, I was one of the best.

Most amazing of all was that my small stature and short, thick legs were sought-after qualities. People actually valued the body that I had hated my entire life. The problem was that they valued it for reasons that weren't in my best interest. You see, small guys with short, thick legs were less likely to break their legs when they jumped out of helicopters in Vietnam.

Even though I knew that I would be going to the U.S. Army Band (known as "Pershing's Own") in Washington, D.C., I threw myself completely into basic training. I did 100 push-ups every night before I went to bed. I volunteered for every possible extra assignment.

I was living inside my body. I could ask things of my body, and it would respond. I could dive at a rope ladder on the "confidence course" and know that my grip would hold. I could crawl under barbed wire with live machine-gun rounds flying just over my head and know I could handle it.

My body—the very same body that had disappointed me my entire life—was now rewarding me. The more I demanded of it, the more it rewarded me. It felt as though there were no limits for me. No walls too high, no distance too far, no challenge too great.

In my college life as a musician, I had encountered the world as a musician. I heard connections between and among sounds that other people didn't hear. I reacted to rhythms. I sensed the timing, the nuance, the elegance of the relationships between the printed notes and the notes played.

I understood the importance of consonance and dissonance and the beauty of the juxtaposition of their elements. I knew what sounds resonated and what sounds did not. And I knew why. I lived always and only inside my head.

During those months in basic training I lived outside my head. I lived in my body. I encountered the world with my body. I felt the world with my hands, heard the world with my ears, and traversed the world with my feet. I got hot. I got cold. I got tired. It was real. It was honest. It was true.

When I left basic training I vowed to stay in shape for the rest of my life. I understood how good it felt to be in a body that you could trust, and I was committed to living my life in that body. For three months after basic training I did just that. Then life intervened.

The only thing worse than never having been an athlete is having been one and given it up. In the years after basic training I gave up my right to be an athlete. I gave up my right to live in my body. I treated my body as if it were disposable; as if when I had used and abused it enough, I could order a replacement. I drank too much. I ate too much. I smoked too much. And I moved too little.

I had no real excuse except the excuses that we all seem to have: I didn't have time. I was working two full-time jobs. I was raising a family. I was trying to establish myself in a career. I knew all of that was true.

What I didn't know was that I was killing myself.

At 28 years old, five years after basic training, I was rushed to the hospital on two separate occasions because it seemed that I was having a heart attack. My blood pressure on one of those occasions was 180 over 132.

I had given up on my dream of being an athlete. What was worse, I couldn't see any way out. I couldn't imagine a life that was different than the life I was living. I couldn't imagine a life without the excesses of too much food and drink.

So for me, the next 15 years were like the dark ages. I had some real career success, but at the expense of my body. And as my body grew prematurely old, my spirit aged right along with it.

By my early 30s I was an old man. I was wearing an old man's clothes and living in an old man's body. I couldn't do anything physical without being sore for days. I couldn't walk anywhere without worrying about where I could stop to rest. And I could never do anything for long before I needed a cigarette.

People ask me about those days now and wonder whether I was miserable. My answer is a resounding "No!" If I had been miserable, maybe I would have changed. If I had been miserable, maybe I would have quit overeating, and drinking, and smoking. No, I wasn't miserable in the least. I had everything I thought I could ever want: a good job, a nice house, cars, motorcycles.

I didn't think there was anything missing. The dreams of a young child who wanted to be an athlete were dreams from a lifetime ago. I didn't have time for dreams anymore. I was too busy living my life.

As my dreams died, so did my spirit. The joy that I had felt earlier in my life, even in failure, was gone. I didn't know it, but I was suffocating in my own ambition. I was chasing other people's dreams for me. I was living out other people's plans for me.

I had lost touch with the essential me. The Sand-box Nonnie. The kid on the basketball court. The young boy for whom failure was so devastating, yet his dream still burned.

> *In many ways I had everything I had ever wanted. But I had lost myself.*

The death of my dream of being an athlete marked the death of my dream of a life in which even the most outrageous childhood goals could be set and achieved. There would be no more reaching for the stars, no more high hopes. The death of my dream of being an athlete meant that I was sentenced to a life of sedentary confinement in a body that wouldn't, and couldn't, make dreams come true.

In many ways I had everything I had ever wanted. I had achieved musical success as a performer, I had a home and a family, and I had a garage full of motorcycles. But all the security and toys and career success that I had in those days were nothing compared to what I had lost. I had lost myself.

PART II

The Adult-Onset Athlete

FIVE

RELEASE FROM SEDENTARY CONFINEMENT

Like so many of us, I spent most of my 20s and 30s trying to get established in a career, get started on a family, and find my way through the vagaries of adult life. Like so many of us, as I entered my 40s I realized that the dreams of my youth had slipped away and that something like middle age was staring me in the face.

I arrived at age 40 as an overweight, overeating smoker who drank more than he should. I was well into a second marriage and well into a third career choice. I crossed the threshold into my 40s as a reasonably happy fat guy with no thought that life could be any different than it was.

The sad truth was that I didn't know any other kind of lifestyle *was* available to me. I was from an era when "fat is where it's at" made sense, and successful people were referred to as "fat cats."

I spent years trying to get jobs with bigger salaries so I could buy bigger houses with bigger garages into which I could put bigger cars. I also bought bigger clothes to go around my bigger waist.

It wasn't as if I was living on the planet Xenon. I knew that smoking and drinking and overeating weren't good for me. I just hadn't had much success changing.

Like most people, I'd been through the dieting and weight-loss drama many times. I'd lost weight to get married. I'd lost weight to apply for a new job. I'd lost weight to go to a high school reunion. But every time I lost the weight, I found it again!

Women aren't the only ones who have closets with multiple sets of clothing. I had my fat clothes; I had my skinny clothes—I even had some pants that had fit when I'd gotten out of army basic training. Those I kept just to remind me of how good I *could* look if I ever wanted to again.

I tried every imaginable kind of diet. I ate nothing but hard-boiled eggs and tuna in water. I drank glass after glass of some vile concoction that was supposed to clean out my intestines. I tried low-carb, no-carb, high-protein, no-protein, good-fat, and bad-fat diets, all of which worked fine until I started eating again.

The real problem, it turned out, wasn't the food I was eating; it was my relationship with the food I was eating. You may not think of yourself as having a relationship with food, but trust me, we all do.

I grew up in an ethnic family environment in which food was everything. Food was love. Food was comfort. Food was reward. *"Mangia, mangia,"* my grandmother would say. Eat, eat. In true Italian fashion, she would serve a pasta course first, then put out a roast ham, sweet potatoes, and all the fixings as the main course, then serve the salad, all followed by fresh cannoli or some equally impressive dolce for dessert.

In my grandmother's world, food was the answer to every question and was the perfect complement to every situation. Someone gets married? Bring on the food. A child is born? Bring on the food.

Even death wasn't an escape from the constant barrage of food. If you've ever been to an Italian reception following a funeral, you know what I mean. We all ate as if we were going to be the next person to die.

It shouldn't have surprised me, then, that as I got older and started making my own food choices, I would gravitate to the foods of my childhood. And it shouldn't have surprised me that I would use food as medication for whatever was bothering me at any given time. Food was, after all, the perfect medication.

It was readily available, relatively cheap, and never in short supply.

In addition to the emphasis on food, I had to contend with the reality of my DNA. We are all a composite mix of our family's genetic features. We have our father's feet, our mother's hands, and our aunt Betty's ears. We can't escape our bloodline.

I come from a long line of "round people." Nearly everyone in my family is short with a big belly. There was little chance that I was going to end up tall and thin with broad shoulders.

The truth of all of this was made clear in an incident that, looking back, should have motivated me to change my life right then and there.

I'm a very casual-dressing person and always have been. I've never liked the suit-and-tie look. Even when I had jobs in which I was required to wear a jacket and tie, I always tried to find ones that *looked* casual.

I had been invited to a fancy dinner party. The dress code for men was tuxedoes. Not owning a tux, I decided to rent one. So, at 43 years old and over 240 pounds, I made my way to the local tuxedo-rental store.

As luck would have it, the daughter of a colleague was working that day. She was a 17-year-old high school student. I, of course wanting to appear as fit as possible, immediately sucked in my belly when I saw her approaching.

She greeted me and explained that she needed to take a couple of measurements before we could pick out the tux. First she measured my outseam, which was 40 inches. Next it was time to measure my waist.

"Dr. Bingham," she said, "you'll have to relax your stomach muscles for me to get an accurate measurement."

Busted! With a huge sigh I released a tidal wave of belly fat that nearly knocked the poor girl over.

With what I noted to be great effort, she reached around behind me and brought the tape measure together in front. "Forty inches," she pronounced loudly enough, I thought, for the entire store to hear. Forty inches.

I was 40 inches by 40 inches from the waist down. I was a cube!

Food was the perfect medication: readily available, relatively cheap, and never in short supply.

You might think the horror of that experience would have been enough to send me home committed to a healthier lifestyle. You'd be wrong. I was so troubled by the experience that I went home and had a cigarette and a beer. That was my solution.

So there I was. I had everything I had ever hoped to have, yet I still felt that somehow something was missing. Furthermore, it was a feeling that I couldn't eat or drink or smoke away. I didn't know what it was, but I knew that if I didn't find it I would never be truly happy.

I was associate dean of the Oberlin College Conservatory of Music at that time. It was a high-profile job with a lot of responsibility. Part of that responsibility was maintaining the conservatory's instrument collection, particularly the Steinway pianos. Oberlin had the largest number of Steinway pianos outside the Steinway factory. The care and maintenance of these instruments were a very serious business.

The number-one piano technician was an avid cyclist. I would see him biking to work and knew that occasionally he took longer rides during the day. I made twice the salary he made. I lived in twice the house. I had more cars, more money, more *everything* than he had—yet he always seemed happy, and I almost never did.

From time to time, in the middle of the day, I would see him ride past my office window. An hour or so later I would see him come back, clearly having exerted himself. Something about all that bothered me, so I called him into the office. I explained that I couldn't have him out riding his bicycle in the middle of the day when we had so much work to do. I explained that faculty members were complaining and that, to protect my job, I simply had to insist that he *not* ride during the workday.

He looked at me and explained that when he got stuck on a problem, the best way for him to find the solution was to go for a ride. If he was tired or frustrated or annoyed, he would go for an hour's ride, and when he came back his mind would be clear. He explained that he was a better employee, doing a better job, because he took time out in the middle of the day to ride.

I didn't have an answer for him. We produced over 300 performances during the school year. He and I, and my whole staff, worked seven days a week for the 15 weeks of the semester. I had not in fact heard any complaints; it just bothered me that he was so content and I was not.

Thinking that maybe he was on to something, I decided to try cycling. I was, after all, a die-hard motorcyclist, and the bicycle would provide the same kind of motion; I'd just have to provide the power with my legs.

I searched local yard sales and came up with what I thought would be the ideal bicycle: a $75, steel-framed, 10-speed Peugeot. This was not one of the fancy index-shifter bikes like you find today. This bike had friction shifters on the downtubes. You either knew what gear you were in or you guessed.

Since I had never owned a 10-speed bicycle before, I didn't have any idea how one went about riding such a machine. The best I could come up with was that you found a gear you could handle and pedaled around in that gear until your legs got stronger; then you went to the next-hardest gear. I figured once I'd gone through all 10 speeds, I'd have to find a bike that had gears 11 through 20.

Things were actually going pretty well. I figured out how to put air in the tires; I learned how to use the brakes; I even tried putting my hands on the lower part of the handlebars every now and then. I was riding—and, amazingly to me, I was enjoying it.

Then the piano technician came for a visit.

His first question was "What's your cadence?" My cadence? I had no idea what my cadence was. I didn't have any idea how to find out what my cadence was. I just got on and pedaled.

"You need to know your cadence or you'll blow out your knees," he told me. What? "If you don't keep your cadence over 90 you'll blow out your knees," he repeated. *Blow out my knees?* Oh, no, not that.

"All right," I told him, "I'll find out what my cadence is, but what do I do if my cadence falls below 90?"

"Change to a lower gear," he told me.

I looked at him as if he had two heads. "What do you mean, change gears? While I'm *moving*?"

"Yes," he said.

I was pretty skeptical, thinking I could never manage to do that.

He started explaining how I should be pedaling, how I should be pushing forward and down and then pulling backward and up.

"How do I keep my foot on the pedal when I'm pulling backward and up?" I asked.

"Ah!" he said. "I brought these for you!" And he pulled out a pair of toe-clips.

Have you seen toe-clips? I'm pretty sure they were used in medieval prisons to keep criminals from escaping. He installed them on my bicycle and told me to go out and try them. Disaster was just minutes away.

I managed to get my feet jammed into the toe-clips all right. It was just that there was no way I could get my feet back out, a fact that became relevant as I approached the first stop sign. In total panic I rolled through the stop sign with my feet firmly attached to the pedals. At the same time I was also trying to reach down between my legs, which I couldn't move because my feet were in the toe-clips, to change to a lower gear.

I steered my way toward a grassy area, coasted to a stop, and fell off the bike.

> *Even though I had been living a life
> of sedentary confinement,
> I had the power to release myself.*

It took several more embarrassing moments, but eventually I worked it all out. I bought a pair of bicycling shoes that made it easier to get in and out of the toe-clips, and I even learned how to shift gears smoothly while pedaling. I was riding. And I was having fun.

I found myself riding nearly every day. I spent the better part of that fall pedaling around rural northern Ohio, enjoying sights, sounds, and smells that I had never known existed. As I got more comfortable I ventured farther and farther from home, and the more I rode, the better I felt.

The piano technician was right about riding in the middle of the day. I would take off at lunch, go ride for an hour, and come back feeling like it was a brand-new day.

I was discovering the joy and magic of an active lifestyle. I was discovering that even though I had been living a life of sedentary confinement, I had the power to release myself.

Much to my amazement and amusement, my body started to change in response to the new activity. I began to have obvious calf muscles. I could see them. I not only felt better, but I looked better too.

Then came another surprise. I began to make better choices about what I was eating. At some level I understood that overeating wasn't going to make me a better cyclist.

It wasn't much of a start, but it was the beginning of what turned out to be a whole new lifestyle. And it all changed again when I bought my first pair of running shoes.

SIX

HITTING THE ROAD

The story of my first days as a runner is one I've told a thousand times, yet I am still surprised by the way it ends.

I'd been cycling for several months and really enjoying it. I'd found a freedom and a joy in the movement that I had never thought possible. It wasn't always easy, but it was always fun, and at that point of my life, knowing I could look forward to an hour of fun a day was enough motivation to keep me pedaling.

Part of my job as associate dean at the Oberlin College Conservatory was to go on remote-audition trips. Along with the director of admissions, I traveled to various cities throughout the United States to hear students who wanted to audition for admission to the conservatory but who could not come to campus. We would be gone for several weeks.

As the trip drew near that first fall after I had started cycling, I worried that if I stopped exercising for that long I'd lose all the fitness gains I had achieved to that point. I knew I needed something simple. Something that didn't require a lot of equipment, and something that I could do wherever I was.

The answer was clear: I would become a runner.

I didn't know anything about being a runner. I knew less about being a runner than I had known about being a cyclist, and you remember how well that had gone. But I was enthusiastic, and that was all that mattered.

Not knowing there were such places as running specialty stores, I went to the same place where I bought my underwear and tires: the mall. After a quick search of the directory, I found myself standing in the doorway of a shop containing what seemed to be the largest collection of athletic shoes I had ever seen in my life. There were shoes of every description and shoes for every imaginable activity. There were shoes of every possible color and color combination. I was overwhelmed.

When I was growing up in the 1950s there was no such thing as a running shoe. There were gym shoes. Period. You wore them during gym class, and that was that. You never wore gym shoes anywhere except the gym. That was why they were called *gym* shoes.

And there were only two brands of gym shoes that I had ever heard of: Keds, with the little blue rectangle on the back of the shoe that you could carefully pull off as the shoes got older, and P. F. Flyers, with the black rectangle on the back. For reasons that are still unclear to me, I always had Keds. I knew kids who had P. F. Flyers, but in my house we were Keds people.

> **I didn't know anything about being a runner.
> I was enthusiastic, and that was all that mattered.**

Not only were there only two brands of shoes that I knew of, but each of those brands produced only two kinds of shoes, as far as I could tell. Your only choice was whether you wanted high-tops or low-tops. That was it.

The athletic kids all had low-tops. We were sure that was why they could run so much faster. They had the lightweight, high-speed, low-top shoes. Not I, of course. The short, pudgy kids wore high-tops. We wore them, our mothers told us, because we needed support for our ankles. Apparently mothers believed that the strain of tumbling and square dancing was severe enough that one could hurt one's ankle.

But there I stood at the mall, looking at, by my guess, nearly 10,000 pairs of shoes. And I, of course, had no idea what I was looking at, or looking for.

As luck would have it I was wearing an old pair of running shoes. Someone had given them to me years earlier, and I wore them when I mowed the lawn or changed the oil in my car or just worked in the garage. They were torn and stained and worn down to the threads.

A nice young man approached me and asked politely if he could help me. I smelled of cigarette smoke and beer, but I proudly pointed at my worn, stained shoes and announced, "I need to replace my running shoes."

That was a mistake. The first question he asked was whether I was an overpronator. I stood there, shocked, and told him I didn't know what that meant but that I was pretty sure it was none of his business. I just needed new running shoes.

He continued the inquisition. How many miles a week was I running? Did I need medial support? Did I want a cushioned shoe? Did I want air or grid or gel? Did I want a training shoe or a racing shoe?

There was something inherently awkward about a highly respected, middle-aged associate dean having to ask for help from an adolescent boy. I looked him square in the eye and said, "I need a left shoe and a right shoe." He started to tell me that he'd go grab a few models and sizes for me to try on, but I stopped him and said I'd take the blue-and-white pair in size 8½. He started to explain that running-shoe sizes were different than those for dress shoes, but I stopped him again and told him to bring me the blue-and-white shoes in 8½ and we'd be done.

He complied, and I walked out with a brand-new pair of running shoes that were the wrong shoes for my running gait and foot motion and were at least one size too small. I had a lot to learn.

I couldn't wait to try them out, so when I got home I decided that I would begin my running career on that very day. The temperature was in the mid-40s, so I knew I needed to wear something to keep me warm. After all, I didn't want to be uncomfortable on my first day as a runner. I grabbed a pair of cotton tube socks and found an old pair of cotton sweatpants, an old cotton t-shirt, and a cotton sweatshirt. I completed the outfit with a jacket, wool cap, and winter gloves. I tied my wrong pair of shoes too tightly and headed out into my new life.

As I stood there on my driveway, it occurred to me that I had no idea what to do. I had never talked to a runner. I'd seen runners occasionally, and none of them ever looked happy. And they never, ever showed old, fat guys running on television. I was going to have to figure it out for myself.

My plan was to run as fast as I could for as far as I could, then repeat until I had run as far and as fast as I wanted to. With a primal scream I set out down my 50-yard stone driveway, headed toward the street at full speed. That first run lasted about eight seconds.

Suddenly I found myself bent over, gasping for breath, wondering how in the world I had ever gotten to the point where I couldn't run more than eight seconds without feeling like I was about to die. What was I going to do now?

I owned nine motorcycles, two cars, a Volkswagen camper, a garden tractor, and even a gas-powered weed whacker. I was in no danger of overexerting myself.

The life I knew was behind me. The abyss was in front of me.

This was the moment of truth, and I think many adult-onset athletes experience a similar moment. It's one thing to make the decision to live a more active life. It's quite another to keep acting on that decision after you've discovered just how far you let yourself go.

I stood there for a while to catch my breath and to decide what to do next. I could turn around and go back to my comfortable life, or I could go forward into the unknown. I chose to go forward, and, in the words of Robert Frost, that has made all the difference.

Realizing that charging ahead at full speed wasn't going to work, I walked some and jogged some and even tried running again some. I stumbled and panted my way as far as I thought I could possibly go and then turned around.

When I turned around I saw that I hadn't even gotten out of sight of my house. All that effort and I could still see my house.

I didn't know it at the time, but that very first day I showed signs of having a runner's mentality: When I got back to my garage, I got into my car and measured how far I had run.

It wasn't much of a start, to be sure. But it was a start. Every day or so I'd lace up my shoes and try it again. Every time I ran I tried to go just a little bit farther than I had the time before.

What I knew for sure was that even though I was awful at it, I liked running. It was pure. It was honest. It was simple. It was just me and my feet and the road.

Those first few months as a runner were not without their problems. When I ran—or did what I called running—on the roads, I was embarrassed if someone saw me and thought I was trying to run. So when a car approached I'd bend down as if I were looking for something until it was out of sight.

But I kept at it. Little by little it got easier. Little by little I was able to go farther until one day I decided I needed a real goal, so I painted a line on the road 1.5 miles from my driveway—1.5 miles out, 1.5 miles back. Three miles. Perfect. I was sure 3 miles was as far as any sane runner would ever want to go. And I can tell you today, after 45 marathons and countless other long-distance events, I still think 3 miles is as far as any sane runner should run.

> *I had discovered the fountain of youth: being active.*

It took the better part of six months to get to that line. Six months of going for it and failing to get there. Six months of failing. At least, that's the way some people might define it. But I didn't feel that I was failing. I felt that I was getting closer to my goal every day, and that was what kept me going.

Then came the historic day. It was spring; I'd been running consistently for months; it was a beautiful day; and, as usual, I decided I would run to the line.

When I got there and turned around, it seemed as if I was miles away from my house. Even when I got close enough to see the house it seemed as if there was no way I could ever get there. One foot after the other, left-right-left-right, I kept moving.

I remember the moment when it occurred to me that I was going to make it. I was elated. During the last few hundred yards it felt as if my feet were barely touching the ground. I sprinted the final yards and stood triumphantly at the end of my driveway, feeling as though I had just won an Olympic gold medal. I had never felt anything like it.

I felt so good that I walked into my house, sat down on the sofa, popped a beer, and lit a cigarette.

It's true that I was making better choices in my life. But it's also true that I had so many bad habits that I wasn't able to quit them all at the same time. I did eventually, but it took years.

I spent the rest of that spring alternating between running and cycling. I bought a better bike and some padded cycling shorts. I even bought a cycling jersey with pockets on the back. I bought a pair of running shoes that fit and a pair of running shorts and running socks. I was into it.

I was having a ball. It was like being a kid again. I looked forward to running and cycling the same way that I had looked forward to playing baseball when I was young. I had, in fact, discovered the fountain of youth: being active.

New worlds, new challenges, and new possibilities seemed to be opening up every day. I did a 50-mile ride, overnighted, and rode back. I rode a metric century. My time for my 3-mile out-and-back dropped from over an hour to under 45 minutes. I was getting better, and I knew it.

My weight had come down; I had finally quit smoking; and although I still enjoyed a glass of wine now and then, I wasn't coming home every day and having a beer or 12. I was changing.

I was becoming something I had always wanted to be. I was becoming an athlete. And the best part was that I could be an athlete all day every day. In fact, the only time I didn't feel like an athlete was when I was running or cycling.

You see, when I was running and cycling, the truth about how I had lived my life was on full display. The evidence of all the years of indiscretion didn't disappear overnight. Much of the evidence never disappeared, even years later. The extra skin that I had developed to cover the extra 100 pounds of me was still there, just in case I needed it again. The emotional fear that I was somehow an athletic imposter still haunted me.

I understood that I couldn't undo the damage from the life that I had led, but I certainly could be both more and less than what I was.

As exciting and fulfilling as all this was, it was nothing compared to what was coming next. I was about to discover what it meant to be a competitor. I was about to go racing.

SEVEN

OFF TO THE RACES

Nothing in my experience as an athlete changed my life more than competing in my first race. I use the word "competing" as a euphemism for what really happened at that first race, which is that I started and finished under my own power without requiring medical attention.

I was about to undergo the biggest professional change of my career. After four years as the associate dean of the Oberlin College Conservatory of Music in Ohio, I was moving to become the chair of the music department at Middle Tennessee State University in Murfreesboro, Tennessee, just outside Nashville. The change in jobs was provoked, in part, by wanting to live in a geographic area where I could more comfortably run and cycle year-round and, in part, by the desire to find a job in which I wouldn't have to work 16-hour days and seven-day weeks—also so I could run and cycle more.

On the weekend that I was to go to Murfreesboro to look for housing, the husband of a friend and fellow doctoral student at the University of Illinois asked if I'd like to go to a race with him. He was a few years older than I and at the time had completed something on the order of 70 marathons and several Ironman® triathlons. We had never met, but I was certain he would not look as middle-aged and unathletic as I did.

It turned out that he did. He was, by his own admission, a back-of-the-packer. He delighted in telling the story of riding a Huffy bicycle in his first Ironman. I figured no matter how slow I was, he was going to be right there beside me.

He told me that on the weekend I would be visiting there was a race called a duathlon that we could sign up for. Not having any idea what a duathlon was, I naturally said I'd love to. Only after I had made the commitment did I have the sense to ask him what we'd be doing.

This duathlon, he explained, was a 5K run followed by a 25K bike followed by another 5K run. I had just run 3 miles for the first time about a week before this conversation, so, needless to say, I was sure I could run the first 5K. Then, with all the resting time during my 25K on the bike, I'd be able to run the second 5K. Ha!

I had no experience in running races or duathlons, but I was a motor sports fan, so I asked him what we'd have to do to qualify for the race. I figured we'd have to get there a day early and demonstrate to the organizers that we were able to compete.

No way, he said. We'd just show up on race morning with our bikes and our checkbooks, and we'd be ready to race. We'd write a check for the entry fee; they'd give us numbers for our bikes and ourselves; and we'd be racers. Wow! All I needed to become a racer was a checkbook. Duathlon sounded like the sport for me.

Sure enough, we got to the race site in Fayetteville, Tennessee, unloaded the bikes, rolled up to the registration table, and handed the nice lady a check for $25. She gave us numbers, and we were all set. She told us to take our bikes to the transition area and then come back for the start of the first run.

At about this point I realized that I had no idea, none at all, what I was doing or what I was about to attempt to do. I didn't have the foggiest idea what the transition area was or what we'd be transitioning into, but I had 25 bucks invested, and I wasn't going to quit before I even got started.

My friend knew what the transition area was all about, so I just followed him to a large parking lot filled with rack after rack of bicycles. All the bikes were painted fancy colors, and they certainly looked faster than my steel Schwinn Le Tour, but I spotted my advantage right away: Very few of the bicycles had actual pedals! They all seemed to have some kind of small protuberance hardly big enough to find with your foot.

And my bike was the only one with a luggage rack.

I was so nervous that I went to the bathroom about ten times while we were waiting. Each time I went, I had to walk by the table with all the trophies and awards. I started to look more carefully at them once my friend explained that I was only competing against men my own age. I wasn't going to have to beat the young guys—just the other old guys like me.

Earlier that week, in preparation for the race, I had run the fastest mile I had ever run in my life. My pace? Twelve minutes. Bearing in mind that I had started at about 25 minutes per mile, I knew I had made a monumental improvement, and I was certain that no man my age could possibly run much faster than a 12-minute mile. So, naturally, I was eyeing the trophies.

I noticed that the start area didn't seem to be all that well organized. I figured that someone would soon get us arranged by age or gender or something. But no one did. In fact, no one seemed to care where we positioned ourselves.

Being a motor sports fanatic, I immediately grabbed the pole position: inside the first row. After all, I knew how fast I was. Surely I was entitled to the pole position if no one challenged me for it.

My friend tugged on my arm and told me to follow him.

"Where are we going?" I asked indignantly.

"We're going to start at the back with no one behind us," he answered.

"Hold on!" I said. "I know that at a 12-minute-per-mile pace, I'm probably one of the fastest guys here, but look, I can't give them that much of a head start."

My friend just laughed and repeated that we would start at the back with no one behind us. Turned out that was where we finished too.

When the start gun sounded, we were left standing there as if we were tied to a tree. I couldn't believe how the crowd of runners just took off. Confused, I looked at my friend.

"What now?" I asked.

"Now," he said, "we start racing."

And we did. We took off at a comfortable pace and began to make our way around the 5K course. Somewhere in the middle an old man was sitting on his porch waving and cheering for all the racers. I gave him a big smile and a wave. It was the first time anyone had ever cheered for me.

As we finished the first 5K, in almost exactly 45 minutes, we found ourselves in a nearly deserted transition area. "Hey," I shouted, stating the blindingly obvious, "there's my bike, and the other bike is yours!" We rolled out of the transition area, mounted our bikes, and headed out on the 25K course.

About halfway through the bicycle leg, we started to notice other competitors heading home. I couldn't imagine that they had finished that far ahead of me, so I assumed they had dropped out.

Nearly an hour and a half after we started the bike leg, we finished. By now most of the competitors were busy packing up and heading for the awards ceremony. Undaunted, we climbed off the bikes and got ready to run the second 5K.

There was only one small problem. When I got off the bike, it felt as if my legs were still bolted to the pedals. It was the strangest feeling. I could see my legs. I knew they were there, but they wouldn't move. I might as well have stuck my feet in cement.

In time my legs loosened up, and we were running—or mostly walking—the course. The old man from earlier in the day was still out on his porch, although he seemed to have lost interest in the race by that point.

"How you boys doing?" he shouted.

"Just great!" I replied.

"Ya know," he said, "'bout everybody else has gone home."

We knew, but we just smiled.

I wasn't racing them. I was racing myself.

He was right, though. Nearly everyone had gone home by then, with the exception of the ambulance driver right behind us. We could hear him on the radio talking to someone: "Yep, they're still moving!"

As we approached the finish line, with the clock on a metal chair and the race director standing impatiently next to it, we picked up our pace. I was overwhelmed with emotion. I was going to finish the race. I wasn't going to win. I wasn't going to place in my age group. But I was going to finish. And for me— the former fat kid, smoker, drinker, overeater—that was all that mattered.

The funniest part of the day actually happened on the way home. I needed to drive back to Ohio right after the race, so I packed up and hit the interstate. A couple of hours later I pulled into a rest area and tried to get out of my car. Every muscle in my body had locked up. I was stuck in the seated position, and there was very little I could do about it.

I had managed to start hobbling my way to the restroom when a man approached and asked if I was all right. I explained that I was in the best shape of my life. He looked at me and said, "Son, if you were in any better shape, you wouldn't be able to walk at all."

But that was it. That was the day my life changed forever. That was the day I discovered a part of myself that I didn't know existed. I was a *competitor*. And I liked it. I liked everything about it. I liked lining up at the start. I liked being out on the course. And I especially liked coming across the finish line. I knew then that my life would never be the same.

> *I discovered a part of myself that I didn't know existed. I was a* competitor.

Running and cycling changed from something I was doing purely for recreation to something I was doing competitively. Everything was different now. I had been transformed from a mild-mannered university administrator to a fierce competitor. I knew that I would find the me I wanted to be deep in the fire of competition.

I started racing every chance I got. I would race two or even three times in a weekend. I would drive 800 miles to run a 5K. It didn't matter that I was finishing last, or nearly last. I was pinning on a race number and putting myself on the line.

I discovered that the running community was full of wonderful people who were all willing to help me. They would give me advice on shoes, on training programs, on race strategies. They would support me when I needed help and encourage me when I was doing well.

I also discovered that some of the hardest-fought battles are not at the front of the field. They are being fought in the back of the pack by those of us with nothing at stake but pride.

I have chased down runners in front of me for miles just because the shorts they wore got on my nerves. I have reached down and demanded more from myself just so I wouldn't have to finish behind someone 20 years older than I. There have been times when I have crossed the finish line spent and exhausted because on that day I was determined not to finish last.

What the faster folks don't always understand is that what binds us as competitors is far more powerful than what separates us by pace. We in the back are often not content with where we are. The competitive juices are flowing through us no matter where in the pack we find ourselves.

To me, that's the magic in racing. I don't know a better way to truly find out who you are than on a racecourse with a number pinned to your chest.

I don't know a better way to discover you've got something left just when you think everything is gone. I don't know a better way to find out what it would take to make you quit, or why you would quit, or even *if* you would quit.

Racing galvanizes our souls, allowing us to escape from the limitations that we put on ourselves and to test the outer limits of our bodies and our spirits.

Even though there was no hope of my winning a race, or even being among the top men in my age group, I loved the act of racing. I loved the spirit of competition.

> *What binds us as competitors is far more powerful than what separates us by pace.*

I found that each race distance presented me with different racing challenges. In the 5K I had to learn how to stay at my physical and emotional limits for the entire distance. In the 10K I had to learn how to pace myself and how to balance my desire to go as fast as I could with the knowledge that I couldn't go all out for the entire distance.

As my race distances got longer, the physical challenges were matched by the emotional and spiritual challenges. When I crossed the finish line of my first marathon, with six people behind me, I cried like a baby. I talk more about this in Chapter 10, but suffice it to say, I don't mean I teared up a little bit—I mean I wept uncontrollably.

I had trained my body to meet the demands of the distance, so I wasn't surprised that I was able to finish. But I hadn't done as good a job preparing my spirit for that first marathon finish. As it turned out, with that final step across that finish line, I erased a lifetime of disappointments for myself. Somehow, that little boy who had missed the winning basket had finally been redeemed.

EIGHT

BLACK TOENAILS
AND CHAFING

You don't have to be very smart to be a runner. It is, after all, simply a matter of alternating feet. There's not a lot of complicated equipment to buy, and most of us have been doing some kind of running all our lives. No, you don't have to be very smart to be a runner—but being stupid isn't much help either.

I have always tried to tell the truth about being a runner. The first truth, it seems to me, is that it is not always about running. Sometimes being a runner is about walking. Sometimes being a runner is, in fact, about not running.

I have also always tried to tell the *whole* truth about being a runner. That is, running will unveil an entire universe of previously unheard-of and unimagined physical conditions. Runners come to know about these things the hard way, through painful experience. I invite you to follow my own uncomfortable journey through this wonderland of physical impairments.

> *Shoes are like love relationships.*
> *What attracts you to the shoe in the first place*
> *may end up being what breaks your heart.*

One word of caution: Runners talk to each other about bodily functions and show each other body parts that are normally reserved only for members of the medical profession. If you have a weak stomach, you may want to skip this chapter.

Let us begin with black toenails. Black toenails, like so many running afflictions, are eminently preventable yet nearly universally experienced. If you haven't experienced the miracle of the black toenail, and the subsequent loss of that toenail, I can predict with a fair degree of certainty that you will.

It starts, or it started for me, with buying a pair of shoes that were too small. It wasn't that they were just a little too small; they were *way* too small. This problem would seem to have an obvious solution: hence the saying "If the shoe fits, wear it." The converse would also seem to be true: "If the shoe doesn't fit, don't wear it."

But shoes are like love relationships. What attracts you to the shoe in the first place may end up being what breaks your heart.

Saucony used to make a shoe called "the Jazz." It was a perfectly fine shoe and was probably absolutely the right shoe for many people. This story is not an indictment of the Saucony Jazz. It is an indictment of my own stupidity and hardheadedness.

When I was a performing musician, I played a lot of jazz. I like listening to jazz. I would go so far as to say that my favorite genre of music is jazz. So of course I was drawn to a running shoe that was called "the Jazz."

It wasn't just that the Jazz model wasn't appropriate for me; the size I bought made it even worse. I knew, or at least I told myself I knew, what a shoe should look like on my foot. Notice I didn't say what it should *feel* like. I had no idea how a running shoe should feel, but I had a vague idea of how I thought it should look.

What I thought was that it should look roughly the same size and shape as my foot. I didn't take into account the fact that as you run, with every foot strike your foot size increases, and over time and distance your foot swells. When running more than a few miles, your foot can expand by up to a size and a half. In other words, if your foot measures statically as a size 8½, it wouldn't be unheard-of for it to measure a size 10 at full expansion. Getting the idea?

I trained for and ran my first marathon wearing a pair of size 8½ Saucony Jazz shoes. The only saving grace was that in preparation for that marathon, I never did a training run longer than 15 miles. I'm not suggesting that approach as a training plan; I'm merely pointing out that my ignorance at that stage of my running career was not limited to shoe choice.

After finishing the marathon I noticed that the toenail on the big toe of my right foot seemed especially sensitive. It wasn't so much an acute pain as a dull throbbing. Since this marathon had been my first, I attributed the pain to the extreme effort and did my best to forget it. After all, the pain that was coursing through the rest of my body was enough to keep my attention.

In a few days the nail stopped hurting. At about the same time it began to resemble a color spectrum that you might see in an elementary school—except this nail was turning colors that you would never find in the *small* Crayola box.

A few days after that, the nail turned a lovely ebony color. I wasn't really worried because it still seemed firmly attached.

But the next day, as I was walking across campus, I felt something strange in my shoe. I took off my shoe and realized that whatever it was, it was inside my sock. When I took off my sock I discovered that it was, as you may have guessed, the toenail from my big toe.

I actually kept that toenail for a long time as a reminder that I need, you need, we all need at least a thumb's width between the ends of our toes and the ends of our running shoes. Even if the shoe looks like a clown shoe to you at first, you must give your foot room to expand. Either that, or put a bowl in your closet to collect your black toenails.

One other word of caution about toenails: You cannot cut them carefully enough before a long run. At mile 18 of the Marine Corps Marathon, I looked down and noticed that my left shoe was a patriotic red, white, and blue. My right shoe was the nice blue and white that it had been at the start. The red on my left shoe was blood.

I was too frightened to take off my shoe at that point, since I had no idea what I might discover, so I ran gingerly for the final 8 miles before I had the courage to look. After removing the red shoe and equally red sock, I found the problem. The toenail on my smallest toe, which I had ever so carefully clipped straight across, had poked a hole in the toe next to it that was squirting blood with every step. That was the day I learned that toenails must be clipped with rounded corners.

Chafing is another subject with which I am quite familiar. I have become a firm believer in the adage that anything that *can* chafe *will* chafe. Parts of your body that you cannot believe are able to rub against other parts of your body indeed can, and will.

For those of us whose DNA has gifted us with somewhat thicker thighs, the bane of our existence is the ever-present danger of "chub rub." If you have to ask what chub rub is, then you've never experienced it. If you know exactly what I'm talking about, read on.

Chub rub is the relentless scraping of the inner thighs against one another. The exact experience differs for different individuals. For some, the chub rub is just a few inches of loose flesh. For others, the rub extends to just above the knee. You know who you are.

There is no miracle cure for chub rub. Scientists and medical researchers have not taken it on with the same enthusiasm that they have for other maladies. My theory is that it's because most scientists are skinny and have never experienced chub rub.

There are some antichafing balms that do a pretty good job of mitigating normal cases of chub rub. You rub the balm on the offending inner thighs to protect the skin. That's fine and dandy for folks with moderate chub rub, but for those of us with more severe cases, the only solution is compression shorts. If, like me, you're not that interested in showing up in public wearing nothing but compression shorts, then cut the lining out of regular running shorts and wear them over the compression shorts.

Trust me.

I've seen close to half a million people finish marathons and half-marathons, and the ones to whom my heart goes out most are the men who finish with two bright streaks of red running down their shirts. The pain that they will experience when they turn around in the shower later that day is almost impossible to describe.

> *Parts of your body that you cannot believe are able to rub against other parts of your body indeed can, and will.*

I was running a marathon in Dallas on a warm, dry day and could feel the beginning of the dreaded nipple chafe. I stopped at every medical station to grab as much Vaseline as I could get on my hand and coated my nipples. I even filled my navel with it just in case I needed more before the next aid station.

A quick word of warning about petroleum jelly and aid stations: Make sure to look carefully at what you're taking. I once saw a participant put a handful of Vaseline into his mouth, thinking it was some kind of energy gel. I'm sure he didn't have to worry about hairballs for a while, but I can't imagine that it helped his performance.

There is an entire litany of annoyances large and small that come into your life as a runner. We haven't even begun to talk about bodily functions and the glory of being regular. The point is that we, as long-distance athletes, have the privilege of thinking about these things.

Over the years I've come to understand that coping with these annoyances helps to make us a part of the running community. It's what separates us from the rest of the world. It's what makes us *us*.

It's also what makes us, in my view, more fundamentally human than people who have never experienced such problems. I used to spend days and weeks worrying about things that really didn't matter at all. I'd fret and plan and connive, trying to control or anticipate some particular outcome.

When I'm running, my problems are immediate, and they are real. They are hard to ignore; they can't be put on the back burner; they can't be delegated. They must be addressed quickly, and I have to get the solution right.

It's one of the great lessons that I've learned through running: Problems happen. Challenges must be faced. For most of my life before I became a runner, I would try everything except facing a problem head-on and tackling it with courage.

As a runner, I don't have any choice but to face my problems. If I'm hot, I have to find a way to cool down. If I'm fatigued, I have to find a way to rejuvenate myself. If I'm injured, I have to find a way to heal.

Being a runner has made me a fundamentally more honest person. Because I have become more honest with myself, I have, by extension, also become more honest with other people.

I cannot lie to anyone about how fast I am. If they are running next to me, they will know. I cannot lie to anyone about how far I can run. When I need to stop, they'll know.

I have also come to realize that other runners are honest with me too. I can't lie about my pace, but neither can they. You can't pretend to be a runner. You can't buy something that represents speed and expect anyone to be impressed.

As a runner, I am less inclined to think I know what's best for someone else, and I am also less inclined to believe that they know what's best for me.

The late George Sheehan wrote that we are all an experiment of one. That's true. But we are also an experiment of one within a community of thousands of experiments.

Through running I have learned to respect my own journey and the journey of others. The pain I have experienced along the way has taught me the compassion to appreciate the pain that others are experiencing.

I have become a part of something—the running community—instead of feeling apart from the world in which I am living. As I have discovered and disclosed my own struggles, I have found others who share the same struggles.

I know now that there is a truth to who I am that connects to the truth of who others are. Not a bad return on the investment of a couple toenails.

PART III

The Glory Years

NINE

COLLECTING T-SHIRTS

The biggest problem I had as an adult-onset athlete was that my closets weren't big enough to hold all the race t-shirts I was collecting. Every race gave out t-shirts, mostly cotton in the early years and technical shirts later on. Every shirt had a story, and none could simply be given away or—dare I say it—thrown away.

Some shirts, of course, meant more because the events themselves meant more. The long-sleeved cotton t-shirt from my first half-Ironman triathlon was reserved for special occasions such as marathon expos. When I wore it everyone knew, or I hoped everyone knew, that I wasn't just a marathoner; I was also a triathlete.

The shirts came to define me as an athlete as much as the training did. Once I had a decent collection of t-shirts I could decide who I wanted to be that day, or what kind of athlete I wanted other people to think I was that day. If I was feeling like a long-distance athlete, I might drag out my Marine Corps Marathon finisher's shirt. If I was feeling a need to connect with other runners around me, I might drag out one of my favorite local race t-shirts, like the one from the Franklin Classic or the Tennessee Park Series.

What the shirts did, as much as anything, was identify me as a part of a community. I was a runner. I belonged. I'm a big motor sports fan—I like NASCAR, IndyCars, Formula 1, you name it. I understood why someone would wear a t-shirt with the number or image of his or her favorite driving personality emblazoned on the back. Like me, they wanted to belong.

> **You don't have to win a race
> to feel like you've won.**

In an odd way, getting t-shirts became the driving force in my training. I was like a coin collector. I had to have shirts from all the distances that I had run.

The other great aspect of t-shirts is that they never identify you by your finishing position or your age group. When I wore my Panama City Half-Ironman shirt, no one knew that I had finished dead last, nearly four hours after the winner. So I began chasing t-shirts instead of trophies.

I was very lucky to live just outside Nashville, Tennessee, at the time that the racing bug really bit me. Tennessee has a wonderful series of state park runs that are held throughout the winter months.

The distances for the state park races varied between 4 miles or so and about 9 miles. The races were never big; usually about a hundred people entered one, give or take. There was no electric timing or official photographers. These events were just a bunch of folks getting together for a race.

For those of you not familiar with Tennessee, it's about 500 miles from the west side of the state to the east. Nashville is just about dead center. That meant I could race all over the state.

At most of the races, especially those at either end of Tennessee, the participants tended to be local runners. It wasn't likely that someone living in Memphis was going to drive eight hours to run a 5-mile race in Bristol. But there were other hard-core Middle Tennessee runners besides me who traveled to both sides of the state.

One of those runners was a guy whose name I never knew, even though I saw him at races for years, whom I simply called "the Leprechaun Man." He was always dressed in green: green shorts, green shirt, and in the colder months a green stocking cap. The fact that he was only about 5 feet tall added to the image.

The Leprechaun Man was probably 10 or 15 years older than I was, so my guess is that he was in his late 50s or early 60s at the time. He wasn't fast, although he was faster than I was, and he always had a smile on his face.

Many of the state park runs were hilly—it was Tennessee, after all—and it was in one of those races that I learned a valuable lesson from the Leprechaun Man. He taught me how to run hills.

We were near each other during one race, and I had managed to get a bit of a lead on him going up a particularly steep hill. I dug deep, pumped my arms, shortened my stride, leaned into the hill, and huffed and puffed my way to the top.

When I finally reached the top, exhausted, I allowed myself to relax and just let gravity carry me down the other side. I opened up my stride a little and coasted down the hill.

Behind me I could hear the Leprechaun Man screaming at full volume, "I'm a downhill runner!" He came flying by me as if I were tied to a tree. I must have had 50 yards or more on him as we started up the hill, but he put that and more on me before we reached the bottom.

He wasn't going to waste his energy pounding up the hill. It didn't make sense. The amount of energy that I was putting out wasn't yielding a faster pace; it was just sending my heart rate soaring and my breathing into overdrive.

The Leprechaun Man's approach to this challenge was exactly the opposite of mine. He walked up the hills at whatever pace he could maintain without going into oxygen debt, and then he picked up his pace on the downhill, where gravity became his friend.

I caught him on the flats between hills and started making my way up the next hill the same way I had before: arms pumping, head pounding, gasping for breath. Ten yards past the crest of the hill, here he came again, screaming at the top of his lungs. Again, he went right by me.

This went on for a few more hills until I wasn't able to catch him on the flats and I had to push even harder to pass him on the uphills when he walked. He never looked over, but I knew *he* knew he was outsmarting me. Sure enough, in time I couldn't catch him on the flats or on the uphills, and he was gone.

I'd like to tell you that I learned my lesson from him during that first race, but I didn't. I just became more determined to beat him. It wasn't until years later that I realized that his strategy of energy management was brilliant.

It was also during this t-shirt-collecting, race-every-weekend period that I learned just how competitive I am and how fierce the competition is at the back of the pack. You never get to see these battles on television, but I can assure you that they are as bitter as anything going on in front, and the rivalries are just as intense.

I trained at the same facility as a guy we all called Big Larry, who was every bit of 6 foot 4 and barrel-chested. Big Larry worked out harder than anyone else I have ever seen. He once actually broke a stair machine because he was pushing down so hard.

Big Larry and I raced together for years. We would often line up side by side. Once the gun sounded, though, Big Larry was long gone. It wasn't unusual in the early years for him to be out of my sight before we got to the first mile marker.

Big Larry was the gold standard as far as I was concerned. I tried to imitate his workout ethic even though there was no way to equal his effort. I modeled myself after him. He was everything I wanted to be.

I marked my improvement by how long I could keep Big Larry in sight at the races. If I got to the first mile marker and could still see Big Larry, I knew I was off to a good start. As I got faster, I was able to keep Big Larry in sight for more miles. I was measuring myself against him at every race.

I still remember the first race that I actually saw Big Larry finish. He was well ahead of me, but I was close enough that I saw him crossing the finish line. It occurred to me then that maybe, just maybe, I could beat Big Larry.

Race after race I tried, and I could never stay with him, but I think Larry figured out what I was trying to do. I think he knew I was gunning for him.

At one local 5K, I was determined that this would be the day I'd get him. I had trained well and was feeling strong. We lined up side by side, and when the gun went off, I committed to staying with him stride for stride. And I did. I knew the pace was off the charts for me, but I was going to hang in there. The first 400 yards were a blur. It seemed to me that Larry was picking up the pace, testing me. A half mile into it, I was way outside my comfort zone. My feet didn't seem attached to my legs. We were on fire.

As we approached the first mile clock, I could see the time. We were running at a sub-7-minutes-per-mile pace. I had never even come close to that pace in training. I looked over at Big Larry and said, "I can't run this fast!" He looked over, smiled, and said, "Neither can I."

As we ran past the clock I sensed that Big Larry was about to slow down. Surely he knew that neither of us could sustain our current pace. He looked like he was going to ease up, so I, in a move of good sportsmanship, slowed down myself.

But he *didn't* slow down. He tricked me.

By then it was too late. I had broken my stride and lost my rhythm, and there was nothing I could do but watch Big Larry take off. He had *looked* like he was going to slow down. He had *sounded* like he was going to slow down. He just *didn't* slow down.

I vowed that day that I would beat him. He had not only outrun me, he had outsmarted me. I couldn't tolerate it.

At another 5K a few weeks later, I was ready to take my shot again. This time, though, I had a completely different race strategy. I wasn't going to go head-to-head with Big Larry from the start. I was going to wait and outkick him at the finish.

In the opening mile I fell back just a little and put 5 or 10 people between Big Larry and me. I didn't want him to know where I was, or how close I was. In the second mile I kept the gap even between Big Larry and me. I was running strong, feeling good, and it seemed as if the plan was working. Larry had no idea where I was.

When we made the final turn and I could see the finish line, I knew this was it. It was go time! Big Larry was less than 10 yards ahead of me, with only about 100 yards to go.

I put my head down and gave it everything I had. With about 50 yards to go, I came up on Big Larry. He looked down but didn't say a thing. I had the momentum now and slowly pulled away. I crossed the finish line about 10 yards ahead of Big Larry.

> **You can be beaten and not be defeated.**

When I turned around to see him, I expected to see the same smile I had always seen on his face when he had beaten me. It wasn't there. His head was down. His shoulders drooped. He looked defeated.

It was never the same between Big Larry and me after that race. We saw each other all the time, even raced together on a relay team once, but I had broken some unspoken rule. I wasn't ever supposed to be better than he was.

I learned a lot about myself in those early years of collecting t-shirts. I learned that I liked passing people much more than I liked being passed. I learned that you don't have to win a race to feel like you've won.

I learned that you can be beaten and not be defeated. I learned that you could have a quiet dignity about your own effort, which has nothing to do with anyone else's effort. I learned that comparing myself to anyone else was a fool's game. I could measure myself against the standard set by other people, but I couldn't make them responsible for my progress. I couldn't judge myself by their achievements.

As an athlete, I had to learn to become my own standard. That awareness began to seep into the rest of my life. I couldn't compare my salary, or the size of my house, or the importance of my job to anyone else's in order to know whether or not I was successful.

Racing became a classroom for me, a classroom in which the teachers didn't stand at the front of the room and lecture but instead gave all that they had in full public view. Their sweat and their effort gave greater meaning to mine. We were learning from each other.

Eventually, though, the t-shirt collection got out of control. There simply wasn't any room for more, so I collected them for a yard sale. I didn't just stack them; I went through each shirt and remembered every event as if it had happened that morning.

Late in the day a woman pulled up and asked how many t-shirts I had. I told her there were about 150. She asked how much I wanted for the whole lot.

When I asked why she wanted them, she explained that she had a little car-washing business, and the cotton shirts would be perfect for drying off the windows and cleaning wheels.

I could barely move. She wanted to take 150 memories of the greatest days in my life and use them on greasy wheels and bug-splattered windshields. I was speechless.

Eventually she put $100 in my hand and motioned to her son to start putting the shirts into the bed of their pickup. It was over. They were gone.

TEN

MEDALS AND METTLE

It soon became clear to me that I wasn't going to win any age-group awards unless I entered races like the triathlon in Evansville, Indiana, where they gave age-group awards to the top three and there were only two in my age group. But those races are hard to find.

If I wasn't going to win an age-group award, then I had to find races that awarded medals to people like me whose best efforts were just that: best efforts.

Medals are more permanent than t-shirts. The woman who bought 150 of my race shirts for her car-washing business wouldn't have had the same interest in my medals.

My medals became my prized possessions, and through them I came to understand how seemingly small symbols can come to mean so much.

When I was growing up, my parents' house was filled with small symbols that were mostly mementos of my childhood: the plaster cast of my hand, a Valentine's Day card I'd made myself. Now my home is filled with the same mementos of my son's childhood: the wreath made of rotini pasta that gets hung on the door every Christmas; the rock with felt feet, head, and tail that, if you have enough imagination, looks very much like a turtle. They are prized possessions.

My home is also filled with the mementos of my *return* to childhood—that is to say, my return to a time of play and joy. These mementos are my finisher's medals, my race photos, and even a second-place trophy from a duathlon in which there were only two men competing in the 45–49 age group.

I'm always interested in what other runners do with their medals. I've been to homes where each medal is ceremoniously displayed in a glass-covered case complete with the race number, race shirt, and photo. I admire these displays and think how splendid it would be to have one.

My own medals, however, are hung over my closet doorknob. Why? Because that's where I unpack after a race weekend. I come home, empty the suitcase, and hang the medal on the door. Unceremonious? Sure. But what's really nice is that, as the number of medals has increased, they have become something like a wind chime. Most of the time I don't notice them hanging there. But when I move the door, their clanging reminds me of what I have accomplished.

More recently, after completing so many marathons, I've had to start hanging the medals on both sides of the doorknob. The ribbons are so thick that it's impossible to actually turn the knob. And their combined weight makes me wonder about bolstering the hinges. The last thing I want is the door crashing to the ground in the middle of the night.

Recently I was asked if, after so many marathons, it gets any easier. It might for some, but not for me. Sure, I understand the distance better. I know not to blast off in the early miles, I recognize the brain fade in the middle, and I'm not surprised by the fatigue in the later miles. But no two marathons are ever exactly the same. And the lessons learned in one may be of no use whatever in the next.

The medals serve to remind me of the humility it takes to run marathons. I see the medals from Chicago and Marine Corps in 1997. That was the "year of the double," when I ran them on back-to-back weekends. The idea of running two marathons in less than two weeks ranks very high on the "stupid Penguin tricks" list.

There are seven London Marathon medals. It's the only course I've ever completed seven times and the course that has the most emotional connections for me. One year my aunt, to whom I was very close, died just before the race, and the family waited until I could get back to hold her funeral. So I've always run London with a combination of joy and sorrow.

There is a medal from the half-marathon in Florence, Italy, where I learned how good a banana and hot tea can taste and just how lost you can get if you lose sight of the runners in front of you and don't speak the local language.

> **There are gold-medal performances at every level of running, at every pace, and at every event, every weekend.**

The doorknob holds the memories of the good days and the not-so-good days, of people who brought great inspiration into my life and then faded away. There are memories of cities and streets and thousands of steps taken toward countless finish lines.

When I give clinics and seminars at marathons and half-marathons, I am always quick to remind the participants that everyone who finishes gets the same medal. It isn't as if at some point on the clock the medals change from gold to silver to bronze. I think race organizers have figured out that the amount of effort it takes to complete the distance isn't a function of how long it takes to cover the mileage.

This fact was brought home to me by Frank Shorter, the two-time Olympic Marathon medalist and iconic figure of the 1970s running boom. He remains one of our most distinguished figures. If he and I weren't practically the same age, I would call him a senior statesman of the sport.

I've heard Shorter describe his gold-medal performance in the 1972 Olympic Marathon many times. But no matter how often I've heard the story, I'm always impressed by the passion, dedication, and commitment it took to earn a place on that starting line in Munich.

At a recent seminar, a runner in the audience asked Shorter about Olympic performances. He wanted to know what it takes to get to the Olympics and what it takes to fully seize the opportunity. Rather than describe the racing perspective of an elite runner, Shorter explained matter-of-factly that there are gold-medal performances happening at every level of running, at every pace, and at every event, every weekend.

The mother of three children who decides to take on a marathon must learn to balance her dreams with the needs of her family, just as an elite athlete must do. On race day, after months of training, she'll give her own personal gold-medal performance by running her hardest and finishing in less than five hours.

The chubby teenager who resolves to change his diet and lose weight for his first 5K understands the discipline it takes for any athlete to get across the finish line. And when he finishes that race, his sense of accomplishment may be as strong as that of an Olympic athlete who has just won gold.

The middle-aged man who quits smoking at age 43 and starts running needs the courage of an Olympian to stick to a healthier lifestyle rather than revert to old ways. I can tell you that firsthand. I can tell you that Frank Shorter couldn't have felt any better receiving his gold medal than I did finishing my first marathon.

On a crisp Sunday morning in November 1993, I stood at the starting line of the Columbus, Ohio, marathon. I had actually stood at an earlier marathon starting line, in Memphis, Tennessee, in December 1992. That day was memorable for all the wrong reasons.

My preparation for my first marathon attempt would have been funny if it hadn't been such a disaster. I had been running for about six months or so when a colleague—and marathoner—suggested that I take a shot at running 26.2 miles.

I was, in a good week, running about 20 miles total. And I wasn't so much running as I was running and walking and jogging and waddling. I was moving at a pace that could best be described as glacial.

By the fall of 2002 I had run a few local 5K races and felt like I was beginning to get a handle on the whole training schedule process, though I hadn't picked up a book or a magazine that might have given me any guidance. I was blissfully ignorant of my own ignorance.

What I knew for sure, or thought I knew for sure, was that to be successful at finishing a marathon you had to learn to run on tired legs. It just made sense to me that by 20 miles or so one's legs would get tired, so learning how to keep moving through that fatigue would be a worthwhile skill.

The plan I devised, all on my own, was to, once a week, bicycle until my legs felt like they couldn't move and *then* do my longest weekly run. Let me repeat that: My training plan for the marathon was to bike until I couldn't move my legs and at that point start my long weekly run.

You can see where this is going.

When I have a plan, I am very disciplined about sticking to it. Did the fact that my legs ached all the time, that my knees were so sore I could barely walk up and down steps, that my appetite was gone, that I couldn't sleep, and that I was on the verge of rage all the time make me change my training plan? No way. Not me. I was an athlete. I was disciplined.

I was motivated. I was so overtrained that even my hair hurt. I was an idiot.

I stuck with this plan for most of that fall. I was doing all my long runs on tired legs, so I figured I didn't need to run more than 15 miles at a time in preparation for the marathon. I calculated that my legs wouldn't get any more tired from the running than they did from the biking, so as long as I could run to mile 11 of the marathon, I'd be fine.

As race day approached, it occurred to me that I should probably rest up some to give my body a chance to get strong again. So for one solid week before the marathon, I did nothing. That's right, nothing. I didn't run. I didn't walk. I didn't cycle. I did nothing.

Getting the picture?

Race morning in Memphis was cold and rainy. The friend who had talked me into doing the marathon had decided not to do it, so I was standing there by myself.

Despite the cold temperature and rain, I had decided that I needed to dress like the elite athletes did, so I had on nothing more than a pair of running shorts and a singlet. It was just above freezing. On my best days I was running about a 12-minutes-per-mile pace, and I was standing in the rain in next to nothing.

At the gun, the crowd began to move away from me much more quickly than I had anticipated.

I tried to run, but my legs felt like logs. They were so stiff from a week of doing nothing that they would barely bend.

I forced the issue and began to run. Before I had reached the first mile marker, my knee hurt so badly that I could barely walk, let alone run. A policeman on a motorcycle rode next to me for the next 5 miles to a place where I knew a friend would be waiting. It took me nearly an hour and a half. I dropped out, hurt and discouraged.

So when people ask me how long it took to finish my first marathon, I tell them 11 months.

The disaster in Memphis prompted me to think about my race strategy in Columbus. I devised a run/walk plan, bought a long-sleeved cotton cycling jersey with pockets in the back to carry whatever I needed, and purchased a railroad engineer's hat that I was convinced would amuse and inspire those around me.

The race started well. I was moving at a comfortable pace. The miles were adding up, and with each mile I became more and more confident that I would finish.

The last 3 miles were a struggle, but nothing I couldn't handle. After nearly five hours of running and walking around the city of Columbus, I saw the finish line. I looked behind me and saw one person.

My greatest effort on my greatest day and I was second-to-last to finish.

I crossed that line, exhausted but satisfied. I'd done it. I'd completed a marathon. As I stood there in the finish area I heard, in the distance, the faint sound of a child crying. The longer I stood there, the closer it seemed to be.

It wasn't the sound of a child crying from being hurt or afraid. It was more the gentle crying of a child who is sad. As I looked around to see where the child was, a volunteer grabbed my arm and asked if I was all right.

There was no child. I was the one who was crying.

I cried for the child in me who had wanted to be an athlete but had failed so many times before. I cried for the young boy who hadn't made the Little League team. I cried for the junior high boy who had missed the basketball shot.

I cried for the young man who had broken so many promises to himself and to others. I had disappointed employers, my family, my friends. I couldn't change any of that, but I cried because with that final step, I had erased a lifetime of disappointment in myself.

Running is a wonderful sport. Unlike nearly every other athletic endeavor, it brings every ability level—fast or slow, seasoned or novice—together to share in a common goal: to stand on the starting line and test our strength, our courage, and our spirit.

> *The glamour of the sport belongs to runners at the front of the pack, but the glory belongs to any one of us.*

It may be true that the glamour of the sport belongs to runners at the front of the pack, but the glory belongs to any one of us, regardless of whether we've stood atop an Olympic podium. If we face the obstacles, overcome our fears, and push our limitations, we can emerge victorious. And then, like Frank Shorter, we too can have our gold-medal moment.

Sometimes I think I should put my medals in a place of greater distinction. I think I should have them displayed where others can see them. But then I remember why I wanted those medals in the first place. I wanted them not to show to anyone else but as reminders to me of my own journey, not only as a runner but as a person.

And I prize them, like my son's rotini wreath, not for what they are but for what they mean to me.

ELEVEN

THE NEED FOR SPEED

Sooner or later every athlete wants to be more than he or she is. It's part of being an athlete. We can't ever be truly satisfied with what we have because we're always wondering what we could achieve. For runners, it always comes down to wanting to go faster or farther or both.

One of the most misunderstood aspects of my philosophy about running is that I am somehow anti-speed. It's true that my second book is titled *No Need for Speed*, but that title spoke more to the fact that the challenges, the achievements, and the satisfaction you can get from running can be obtained at any pace.

And it's not that I'm not competitive by nature—I am. But sometimes you just don't realize how competitive you are until you are forced by circumstances beyond your control to either put up or shut up.

For example, consider what I now refer to as the "Old Man with a Big Motor" incident. I was visiting a good friend in southern California. That summer I was traveling around the country in my Firebird, so we went out for a pleasant car ride on a beautiful summer evening. The top was down, the V-8 was rumbling—we were enjoying the experience, and minding our own business.

As we were waiting at a red light, up came a 20-something man in some kind of four-cylinder Euro–sports sedan with loud mufflers. He kept racing his engine, waiting for the light to turn green. It was annoying, to say the least.

I looked over at my friend, and we both smiled. Without saying a word, we knew what had to be done. When the light changed, I gave the young man a lesson in what happens when you put all 300 horses to work at the same time.

Why did I do it? Testosterone? Fear of aging? Mindless machismo? Nope. It's just a kick to blow the doors off someone who challenges you. And it's just as much fun in a road race as it is on the streets of La Jolla.

I admit it. In spite of all my talk about the joy of the journey, at some level I'm a closet competitor. I enjoy passing people. I enjoy beating someone. I enjoy the strategy of setting someone up. I enjoy deciding on the precise moment when I will surge past my competition. I enjoy pushing myself until I know they will not pass me back.

> **I have reached deep into my soul and made deals with the devil to run down just one person.**

Maybe the race number produces this effect. Maybe pinning on a number transforms you from a normal human being into a gladiator. Or maybe it's just plain fun.

Some runners tell me they don't feel competitive, even in races. They try to convince me that they never notice when someone passes them. They even try to convince me that they don't notice when *they* pass someone else. I don't believe them.

I've heard the rhetoric. I've even promoted it. You're not racing against anyone but yourself. You're racing the clock. You're just trying to do your best. All of that is true—in part. But at some level, every runner except the one in the lead is chasing someone.

Still not convinced? Watch the race for last place. Make no mistake, it *is* a race. I know. I've been there. I have reached deep into my soul and made deals with the devil to run down just one person. And I'm embarrassed to tell you that more than once, that person has been a friend of mine.

It's not an age issue. I've chased down youngsters, and I've been run over by senior citizens. During a race nothing matters but how fast *you're* running and how fast *they're* running.

My biggest enemy in a road race is my sense of humor. The mere idea of me and another runner of similar ability racing is often enough to send me into gales of uncontrolled laughter. I just can't get over the absurdity—spending so much effort on deciding who will finish first among the last.

The ferocity of competition can become especially heated if the other person recognizes me. For them, it then becomes not just a matter of beating another runner but of not finishing behind me. No one, it seems, wants to suffer the indignity of finishing behind the Penguin.

In the end, though, it's all a matter of good fun. Unless awards are being given to the top 30 finishers in each age group, I'm really competing only for bragging rights.

I've never looked at another person and said he or she should go slower. I've said that when runners aren't happy with their running and racing, it may be because their expectations are unrealistic, and by simply resetting their goals they could find greater satisfaction. That's true. And it's often true that giving yourself permission to slow down will make you a much happier person.

It should go without saying that we are not all gifted athletes. I am certainly not gifted in any way—a point that has been driven home repeatedly at races over the years. There was even a training incident I recall that might have made a weaker man quit. But I was either too stubborn or too stupid to stop.

I was training for a triathlon. The reasons why I thought I had the time in my life to train in three different sports elude me now, but at the time I was convinced that I could do it. On this particular evening, I was at the pool working on my technique.

Swimming, it turns out, is a sport in which technique is really important. To get through the water quickly, there are some dos and don'ts that must be adhered to. I was trying to learn these guidelines.

A friend and fellow triathlete had been very generous with his time and expertise. He had spent weeks helping me learn the skills needed to be a decent swimmer. He had shown me how to reach out during the stroke, how to pull back, how to finish the stroke, how to breathe, and how to kick.

Together we had spent hours going up and down the pool, and I just wasn't going any faster. Finally

I asked him why he thought I wasn't improving. He looked at me and said, "Maybe you just suck at this."

As it turned out, he was right. I did suck at swimming, but that didn't stop me from participating in a number of triathlons. It wasn't that I didn't *want* to be better; I just wasn't.

I worked for several years with the great running coach Roy Benson. He and I presented weekend running camps aimed at adult-onset athletes. Roy was there because he knew what he was talking about. I was there because I knew what the participants were talking about.

In addition to creating training schedules for participants, we spent time on the track with them to work on form and running efficiency. It wasn't unusual for me to spend most of an afternoon running repeat 400-yard laps with the campers.

After nearly every weekend, Roy would take me aside and tell me that, based on what he had observed me doing, I could be a lot faster than I was. And nearly every weekend I would respond with the same question: "Why?"

Why would I want to be faster? What benefit is there, for me, in finishing a race faster? When I'm out there racing, I'm already doing what I want to be doing, so why would I want it to be over? And if I can control how long I get to do what I want to do, why would I hurry to end it?

Roy never had an answer.

But the truth is that I have run races as fast as I can. I have run races in order to set a new personal record. I have trained and prepared for races in which my only goal was to run as fast as I could. To be honest, those have been some of the most extraordinary moments of my life.

One such moment came at the Sunburst 10K in South Bend, Indiana. I had been running for several years, had completed a number of marathons and half-marathons, and had raced hard in a lot of 5Ks. However, I had never tried to run a hard, fast 10K.

The day was nearly perfect, I was well trained and well rested and eager to take on the challenge of running a fast 10K. For those of you who haven't tried a 10K, I strongly recommend it. It is a magic distance. Running a 10K really well is a work of art and something I've done only once in nearly 20 years of running.

My plan was to run about 30 seconds per mile under my race pace for the first 2 miles, right at race pace for the middle 2 miles, and 30 seconds under race pace for mile 5. Then I'd just go for broke from there to the finish.

As the race began to unfold I noticed that the field was spreading out in such a way that I could pick out runners ahead of me whom I wanted to catch. They seemed to be separating by the exact distances I needed in order to achieve my goal.

Miles 1 and 2 were perfect. I spotted a pair of red running shorts ahead and set out to catch them. Over the next 2 miles I didn't think of anything except catching those red shorts.

As I passed them I picked out a pair of blue shorts up ahead. This would be more difficult. I had picked up the pace quite a bit by that point and knew I was approaching my limit. By the end of mile 5, I had caught the blue shorts and passed them.

Just then a guy who looked to be about my age passed *me*. *Hold on*, I thought. *He's been shadowing me and covering my every move. And now, as we enter the last 1.2 miles, he thinks he's going to pass me? Not today.*

I passed him back. He wasn't happy. He passed me back. I wasn't happy. We kept exchanging the "lead" between us.

The race finished on the track at Notre Dame. As we entered the stadium I pulled away just slightly. I could see the finish line at the other end of the track. I was holding on for dear life. I knew that if he came by me now, I would have no response.

As I made the final turn I could see the clock. I couldn't believe it—it was at 50 minutes. I was going to run a 10K in just over 50 minutes. I finished, officially, in 51:03.

I turned to find the man who had challenged me and who had, with that challenge, helped me find something deep inside me that I had never known existed. He showed me a strength, a determination, and a willingness to suffer that I never knew I had. I wanted to thank him.

He was nowhere to be found. I don't know what happened to him. I don't know if he dropped out; I don't know if he somehow slipped past me in the chutes. I never saw him again. But I remember him to this day and am grateful to him for teaching me how to look into the dark abyss of my spirit and find what I need.

> There is something about trying to get faster that can change you. There's something about finding out where the limits are that can make you defy those limits.

For me, it's never been about some abstract idea of pace. I don't believe that if you can't run at a sub-6-minutes-per-mile pace, you can't race. I've seen runners at a 12-minute pace who I believe have more heart, more race sense, and more sheer guts than some of the world's fastest runners.

There is, though, something about trying to get faster that can change you. There's something about finding out where the limits are that can make you defy those limits. And that's where the need for speed becomes an essential tool for the accidental athlete.

If you accept the labels that others put on you, if you accept that because your pace is slow or your body is ponderous or you are not athletically gifted, you can't enjoy the grandeur of being an athlete, then you are wrong. You can. I know. I have.

What I've felt on the days of my best efforts is no different than what any athlete feels. What matters is that on that day, I have given my all in pursuit of whatever my goal was.

Steve Prefontaine, widely considered to have been one of the greatest runners of all time, is quoted as saying, "To give less than your best is to sacrifice the gift." I couldn't agree more.

He also said, "A lot of people run to see who's the fastest. I run to see who has the most guts." And I agree with that as well.

It isn't pace that separates those who are willing to test themselves from those who are content to be what they are. It isn't speed that makes a person a better runner or a better racer. It's that moment when you aren't sure what you'll find when you reach deep into your guts and discover there's something left.

I am not a competitor to be taken lightly, so consider yourself warned. I'm throwing down the gauntlet. That heavy breathing you hear behind you could be me. Those pounding footsteps could be mine. And if they are, you're in for the race of your life.

TWELVE

LOOKING FOR ADVENTURE

I'm not exactly sure when it crossed my mind that running wasn't enough, that—in a way—running could actually be the base aerobic activity that would allow me to do all sorts of other activities. I'm not sure where it started, but later I will tell you exactly where it ended.

This desire for adventure, for expanding my world beyond what I had experienced, started innocently enough. My wife and coauthor, Coach Jenny Hadfield, and I were vacationing in Hawaii on the island of Kauai. It was early in our marriage, and we were still eager to share each other's interests.

My main lifelong passion happens to be motorcycling, so Jenny agreed that one day we would rent a motorcycle and see the island from a Harley. It was great, and we ended up riding almost 200 miles on an island that is only about 40 miles long.

In exchange for the day of motorcycling, I agreed to hike the Na Pali Coast with Jenny. The only land access to the enchanted area is via the Kalalau Trail, one of the most challenging and treacherous hikes in Kauai because of the narrow sections and muddy topsoil. But I was game.

Because I was a runner, I had every reason to believe I was physically up to the challenge. In the old days, before I became an athlete, I would never have considered anything like this kind of hike. First, I wouldn't have had any way to carry a cooler of beer, and second, I would have had to stop every 30 minutes or so for a cigarette.

But these were different days, so off we went. Jenny was an experienced adventure racer, so it made sense for her to take the lead. I put my male ego aside and let my better judgment prevail. The trail was indeed narrow at times, and muddy, and I'm not embarrassed to tell you that there were many moments when I was afraid.

It was a spectacular hike. The scenery was gorgeous, and the whole experience was one I'll never forget. The most interesting discovery, though, was that I was able to use both the physical and the mental skills I had learned as an athlete to accomplish something I would otherwise have thought impossible.

On another occasion we were visiting Alaska for the Mayor's Midnight Sun Marathon in Anchorage. We stayed a few extra days to experience Alaska on our own. Because Jenny likes to experience the world up close and personal, I somehow found myself paddling a sea kayak in Resurrection Bay on the Kenai Peninsula. Bear in mind that I had only sat in a kayak once before, and that hadn't ended well.

> **The gift of self-discovery is one of the greatest gifts that comes from living as an athlete.**

It was another wonderful day. I saw a bald eagle in the wild for the first time in my life. I tried something I had never done before and enjoyed it. I found that I had the ability to set aside my fear and try something new, all because I was living my life as an athlete.

So far, so good.

The problem with being successful at little things is that it gives you the idea that you can be successful at bigger things. Having hiked in Hawaii and kayaked in Alaska, I was now convinced that there was nothing I couldn't do.

That was why I found myself on a plane flying across the ocean with a backpack, running shoes, cycling shoes, and trail mix, intending to compete in a two-man, two-day adventure race in northern England.

My teammate was the former editor of the *Runner's World* UK edition, Steven Seaton. Steven was an experienced adventure racer and had competed in expedition-length events of nearly every description, including the Eco-Challenge.

I arrived enthusiastic and completely naive about what I was about to face. The Brits, I discovered, are a hardy bunch. Their idea of a fun challenge was my idea of total insanity. We were set to bike, hike, run, paddle, and navigate our way around the English countryside for two days with nothing more than what we could carry on our backs.

It all went well for a bit. It turned out that although I'm not highly skilled at navigation, I don't have a bad sense of it, so we moved slowly but surely through the first hike/run/navigation section. As the day wore on, however, my enthusiasm began to wane—just in time for us to begin the mountain biking stage.

I should, in fairness, point out that I had no idea that the hand brakes on British bicycles are opposite those on U.S. bicycles. It should come as no surprise then when I tell you that in the middle of a fairly steep downhill section, when I grabbed what I thought was the rear brake (which turned out to be the front brake), I managed to fly head over heels onto the ground.

It might have served our team spirit better if Steven had shown a modicum of concern for my well-being—but he didn't. Something to do with the Brits and the "stiff upper lip" business, I suppose. He looked down at my borrowed, now bent, bicycle, and then at me before asking how soon I'd be ready to go on.

That night we slept some, and we got up the next morning for the final two elements: an 8-mile run and a paddle in a two-man inflatable boat.

I was still a bit knackered from the fall and the ride but managed to get through the run pretty well before setting off for the final paddle. I hopped into the inflatable, and Steven pushed off and jumped in. As I adjusted my position I kicked open the relief valve, and the boat began to lose air and sink.

That was the best thing that happened all day.

My paddling skills were awful, despite my recent success in Alaska. In fact, my paddling was so bad that the less I paddled, the faster we went. The more I paddled, the worse it was for Steven until he finally shouted at me to just put the paddle in my lap and sit still.

I adjusted my position again and—you guessed it— kicked open the relief valve a second time.

The English have a peculiar kind of profanity. With the accent, even when they are calling you names and questioning your heritage and your intellect, it sounds like they are saying something nice.

We finished the event, packed our gear in Steven's car, and drove back to London without saying a word.

You might think an experience like that would be enough to make me quit adventure racing and focus on something more straightforward, like training for a marathon or climbing the Empire State Building. But not I. I was living in an athlete's body for the first time in my life, and I was going to experience it all.

By now Jenny had competed in a couple of Eco-Challenges and had done lots of multiday, multistage, multielement races. She convinced me that it might help if I were to learn some of the fundamental skills of adventure racing—paddling, for example—and suggested that I attend a two-day adventure racing camp. I couldn't wait. The best part was that the graduation exercise was a 24-hour, two-person-team adventure race through the wilds of West Virginia. What could go wrong?

In my own defense, I should remind you that I was well into my 50s at that point. I should have known better. I could have known better. But I didn't.

I was the oldest "camper" by about 20 years. The camp director was a former Special Forces soldier who had removed a bullet from his own skull—and showed us the scar to prove it. The same guy told us not to worry about pain. He said the body manages pain all by itself, and if the pain really gets too bad, you'll just pass out.

He told us all this in his welcome talk.

First on the agenda was learning how to rappel. I was strapped into a climbing harness that yanked on parts of my body not designed to be yanked and attached to my butt like a vise grip. I was standing on a cliff with my back to a sheer drop-off and a rope between my legs when I heard a young man say, "Take a step back."

He might as well have said, "Take a saw and cut off your arm." I looked at him in disbelief and told him I had socks that were older than he was, and there was no way I was going to accept that he had secured the ropes correctly—and definitely *no* way I was going to step backward over the cliff under those circumstances.

"Step back and trust the rope," he said calmly. Again I explained that it wasn't about not trusting the rope. I could see the rope. I didn't trust him.

"Step back and trust the rope," he repeated. And I did. I stepped back. The rope tightened in front of me. "Let out a little rope and start to descend," he said. And I did.

I was moving down the cliff face. I was scared to death, but I was moving down the face. I don't know that anything had ever felt as good as the moment when I finally touched the ground. I had reached into the unknown and found that I had more than I had expected.

That afternoon we were taught paddling skills in canoes. My paddling, like my swimming, just isn't where my strength lies, and my canoe partner and I managed to go through every rapids backward. The instructor was impressed with our consistency if not our skill.

The next evening it was time to go racing. I had been paired with Dale, an experienced racer and former marine who had volunteered to be my partner. The moment before the start of that race, as I stood there teamed with him, was one of the most thrilling I have ever experienced. Here I was, a former fat kid, smoker, drinker, and overeater, teamed up with a former marine and getting ready to head out into the West Virginia night with nothing but a compass and a backpack. I was thrilled.

The excitement shifted to terror as the darkness set in. We had maps. We had compasses. We had each other. And I was no help at all.

It adds to the sense of terror when you see head-lamps bouncing around the West Virginia woods, going in every imaginable direction. It's hard to figure out how you can be right if everyone else is wrong.

If hiking in a pitch-black forest is difficult, moun-tain biking in that environment is immeasurably worse. It is sad but true that I never once got on my bicycle during that night. I pushed it the entire way.

With the morning light we were able to ride down the mountain to the river, where we hopped on "boogie boards." My swimming skills transferred perfectly to the boogie board, and the harder I kicked, the faster I went backward.

Eventually, like Steven before him, Dale asked me to please stop trying to help, and he towed me the entire length of the river leg.

As we climbed out of the river, now some 18 hours or so into the race, the fatigue was setting in. We had another long uphill hike, a zip-line back across the river, and then a mountain bike ride on the road back to the camp and the finish line. I was near the end of my energy, and I knew it.

About 22 hours into the race, after we had been hiking uphill for nearly 4 hours, I sat down and took off my backpack.

"What are you doing?" Dale asked.

"I'm done," I said emphatically. "I can't go on."

He laughed. "What do you think happens now? Nobody knows where you are. *You* don't even know where you are. Nobody can come get you, and your truck is at the finish line. How are you planning to get back?"

If there has ever been an epiphany in my life, it was at that moment. He was right. I didn't know where I was, and nobody, but nobody else did—except Dale.

I only had one choice. I stood up, put my pack back on, and started walking up the hill.

It was in that moment that I had the flash of enlightenment. How many times had I gotten to the end of my limits and quit? How many times had I allowed myself to believe that just because I thought I couldn't take another step, I couldn't?

> *My brain said I didn't have anything left.*
> *My will said there is always something left.*
> *You just have to know where to look.*

How many times had I let my head tell my body what it could and couldn't do? How many times had I let my emotions dictate what I was capable of?

Standing up was an act of defiance. It was an act of liberation for my body. It was in the quiet of a West Virginia mountainside that I found myself, even though I had no idea what I was looking for.

We finished. The zip-line went fine, and Dale essentially pushed me on the bike, but we finished. We missed the 24-hour cutoff, but we finished.

The gift of self-discovery is one of the greatest gifts that comes from living as an athlete. I don't know any other way to truly come face-to-face with your own beliefs about yourself.

The war that had been raging in my soul for my entire life came down to that one battle of my spirit versus my intellect. My brain said I couldn't. My will said I had to.

My brain said I didn't have anything left. My will said there is always something left. You just have to know where to look.

PART IV

The Back Nine

THIRTEEN

THE LAST BEST DAY

As we sat backstage at the Scotiabank Toronto Waterfront Marathon a few years ago, the expo coordinator, John Beadle, put an idea into my head that I just couldn't shake. It wasn't one of those ideas that I was glad to have in my head. It was like an arrow in my brain that the doctors were afraid to pull out.

John is a Brit, born and raised in England. He was a pretty fair club racer in his day. Club racing in England is a big deal, and to be successful at it is a very big deal. John hadn't raced in nearly 25 years, not so much because he didn't want to as because his moment of competitive time had past. In John's world racing to win was fun, but racing to finish was not.

The idea that he forced into my head was that we never know what's going to be our last best day. We can't know. The race that turns out to be our last best day can't be recognized in the moment—it can be seen only in retrospect.

Now that I've been running for nearly 20 years, I think it's fair to say that my last best day is behind me somewhere. I haven't spent much time trying to figure out when it was, but I have a few ideas. The difference between my last best day and John's is that mine has nothing to do with my finishing time.

One of the great truths and miracles of getting more active is that even for someone like me, who didn't start running until he was decidedly middle-aged, we have years when, if we're training, we will improve. No matter where we start, if we are willing to work at it, we will get better. And for runners, that means faster.

It didn't hurt that it took me nearly 30 minutes to run/walk/waddle my first mile. When you are that slow to begin with, early improvement comes pretty easily. Little by little I was able to improve my time until I could comfortably run/walk a mile in 15 minutes. I was twice as fast as when I had started. I was thrilled.

I bought the books on getting faster, learned how to pronounce "fartlek" and use it in a sentence without giggling like a schoolboy, and began to get an understanding of concepts such as anaerobic threshold and

VO_2max. I started to speak the language of speed even though I couldn't demonstrate it with my body.

My workouts changed from being delighted that I could run 3 miles to being disappointed that I couldn't run them as fast as I had the day before. I found a local track and started doing speed work, repeats, and ladder workouts. My last best day was still before me, and I knew it.

My racing changed from an activity that nourished me and made me feel connected to those around me in the running community to a self-absorbed activity that nearly always left me discouraged because I hadn't met my goal. I had become one of those runners who nearly always crossed the finish line angry.

Looking back, I can see now that I was missing opportunities to feel great. I let my ego and some predetermined idea of what "good" would be on a given day steal what could have been small victories for me.

I was not alone. Standing at the finish line of races today, I see people come across the line angry with themselves and disappointed with their times. They're grumpy when they finish. There's no joy in their faces.

I want to grab them and remind them that life doesn't guarantee that they will see another start line, let alone another finish line. I want them to be grateful for what they have achieved, not discouraged by what they did not.

Roy Benson, a great friend and wonderful coach, would tell me that there are only two reasons why people should train. The first is to improve, and the second is to slow the rate of decline.

> *Our last best day is*
> *lying in wait out there somewhere.*

He's right, of course. It's just that none of us know when that decline is going to begin. We're so focused on running up the hill of improvement that we don't notice when we've reached the top.

I was improving. My times were getting faster. I had gone from being last, or nearly last, to being solidly in the middle of the finishing field. In my mind, I was happy to have moved up from the back of the pack. I was happy that I had moved from being truly awful to being merely mediocre.

What I didn't know then—what none of us know— is that there is a date on a calendar somewhere already circled in ink, and there's nothing we can do about it. Our last best day is lying in wait out there somewhere.

Where I think I may differ from the John Beadles of the world is that my last best day may have nothing to do with my finish time. I am well aware of the fact that my personal bests at every distance are behind me. I'm not going to find some magic potion that will give me the strength and energy to run my fastest 5K at this point in my life. Those days are gone, and my last best day may already be in the past.

Maybe my last best day was at the Marine Corps Marathon in 2001. The world had just been sent into a state of shock by the attacks of 9/11. The running industry was not immune from the aftereffects, and many races that fall were either severely cut back or canceled.

The Army Ten-Miler had been canceled. The Air Force Marathon had been canceled. So I was a little surprised when the race director of the Marine Corps Marathon called me to say that the race would go on as scheduled. When I asked if he was concerned about safety issues, given the current state of world affairs, he answered, "We're marines."

I wasn't fully prepared to run that marathon that year, but I agreed to start and go through at least the halfway mark. It was important, I thought, for me to demonstrate my willingness to trust that the marines would be ready and able to put on a marathon no matter what else was going on in the world.

There were many who decided not to run that year, but those of us who did line up at the start felt something a little different than usual as the band played the national anthem and the cannon sounded. There was no escaping the fact that this year the world was a different place, and we were running for different reasons.

The course took us past the Pentagon, where the gash in the side of the building was still obvious. My son, who is in the army, had helped with the cleanup and recovery at the Pentagon. I am an army veteran. Running past the destruction and knowing that people had died was sobering.

As I got to mile 13, where I had expected to stop, I found that I couldn't walk off the course. I couldn't step away from the experience of being there, in Washington, D.C., surrounded by runners, as an expression of our beliefs. And I couldn't walk away from the thousands of marines who were there to support us.

So when I finished the full marathon, I made my way to the VIP tent, where, as luck would have it, the commandant of the U.S. Marine Corps was standing. I approached him, planning to simply thank him for putting on such an excellent event. Instead, as I shook his hand and began to speak, my eyes filled with tears. I told him that I couldn't believe he would turn out all the resources at his disposal just so we could run a marathon. Through my tears I told him that, for me, it was part of what defined us as a nation and that we were not going to simply lie down in defeat.

He smiled, in the way that generals smile, and thanked me. Then he echoed what the race director had said: "We're marines."

I had never had a marathon before or since that meant as much to me, that moved me so much, or that made me so happy to be a runner and have the privilege of participating. It was, at the very least, one of my finest hours.

It might be that my last best day was actually two days: the 2006 Walt Disney Marathon and Half-Marathon weekend. I had decided, or rather I had foolishly agreed, to attempt the Goofy challenge, which meant running the half-marathon on Saturday and the full marathon on Sunday. I say "foolishly" because, to be honest, I hadn't given a ton of thought to the prospect of running 31.3 miles in two days. Standing at the start line of that half, I remember thinking, as it says on a shirt I've seen, that this had seemed like a good idea three months before.

From the very first step of the half-marathon, I knew I was in trouble. I had been ignoring an inguinal hernia for months (okay, years). It didn't bother me all the time, and when it did I could usually push it back in, and that was that.

I'm not sure if it was the cold, or having spent hours on my feet at the expo, or some other reason, but with almost the very first step the hernia popped out, and there was nothing I could do.

I would run for a while, then walk for a while, then lie down on the grass for a while. I stopped and turned myself nearly upside down, hoping things might settle down.

Eventually I used my jacket to tie my cell phone against the affected area in a kind of makeshift truss. I literally hobbled my way to the finish line, grimacing with every step. It was, without question, the worst day of my running life.

The question then was, what to do about the marathon? Did I run it? Did I think I could tolerate that pain for twice as many miles? Did it make any sense to even try?

I decided I would line up at the start (I was supposed to address the crowd) and just see how far I could go. I was prepared to step off the course at any time, make my way to an aid station, and hop the bus to the finish.

As I approached the first mile marker I did a quick status update. I actually felt pretty good. I was a little tired from the previous day but wasn't in any pain. I kept going.

Mile after mile after mile I waited for the searing pain to erupt. I looked and listened and felt for the hernia. It wasn't there. I was running some, walking some, and getting through the marathon.

As I crossed the finish line, pain-free, and made my way into the tent to get my Goofy medal, I'm sure there was no one on the planet more pleased with himself and more surprised by the results. It wasn't my fastest marathon by any means, but I haven't run another marathon since that one, which is why I think it may well have been my last best day.

I am literally running for my life.

There are a host of other races that may turn out to have been my last best day. There was the 1999 Rock 'n' Roll marathon in San Diego that I ran with my son. It was a day I'll never forget, and if it was my last best day, I'll take it.

Or maybe my last best day was the 2005 Chicago Marathon that I ran/walked with a friend from New Zealand. We finished nearly 30 minutes earlier than we had predicted, and I was able to spend the time being both tour guide and marathon partner.

But what if, maybe—just maybe—my last best day is still out there somewhere? What if the date circled on that calendar is still years away? What then?

That's where I think a club racer like John Beadle and an aging Penguin like John Bingham separate. I'm not willing to define my last best day as the last fastest day. I'm not willing to concede that my last fastest day was in fact my last best day.

I am literally running for my life. I am running because, for me, the physical, emotional, mental, and spiritual benefits of running far outweigh the struggles, setbacks, and challenges. I am running because, for me, not running is unthinkable. I am running because I am a runner. It's that simple.

If that's the case, then how can I be convinced that my last best day has already passed? How can I continue to find new goals, overcome new obstacles, and experience new successes if my last best day has already come and gone?

There's still so much that I want to do as a runner. There are races that I haven't been able to run that have been on my list for years. There are places where I want to run that I have only read about or seen photographs of.

My life as a runner is still as vital and as interesting to me today as it was the day I started. I didn't know what was going to happen then, I don't know what's going to happen now.

Running has become an act of faith. Running allows me to believe that there is something better out there for me. Running allows me to believe that I can be not just a better runner but also a better person.

Running allows me to believe that if I am willing to work hard enough, I can achieve the impossible. Running has taught me that the limits I place on myself are illusions.

Through running I am learning not just how to run today but how to run tomorrow. My running is a mirror of my life, and my life is a mirror of my running.

I don't believe I have lived my last best day. I don't believe I have run my last best run. My last best day is still out there somewhere, and every day is an opportunity to find it.

FOURTEEN

THE COMEBACK KID

For years every January was the same because every December I finally conceded to whatever injury had been nagging me since—well, since the spring. Because I wouldn't take time off to heal, those little aches that started in May would explode into full-blown injuries by Christmas. I had to stop running until it didn't hurt to walk. So every January I had to start over. And every January I swore that I would be wiser than I had been the year before.

I never was.

When you start running at age 43, as I did, it's easy to forget that while the activity is brand-new, your body isn't. It's also easy to get caught up in how much fun you're having and allow your enthusiasm to get the best of you.

I was one of those people who believed that everything that was written about running injuries applied to everyone except me. I believed that all of the advice about increasing mileage slowly and doing speed work only once a week was for those who were weak in body and spirit.

> *I was just as capable of doing damage to myself by overdoing something good as I had ever been at overdoing something bad.*

I believed that if running 3 miles a day 3 days a week was good for you, then surely running 6 miles a day 6 days a week would be infinitely better.

See, a funny thing happened when I started to run: I started to feel better. Just living my life became easier because I was more active. I also started to change what I ate, eventually quit smoking, and even considered whether having a beer or 12 every day was a good idea.

What didn't change was that I was completely and totally disconnected from my body.

This shouldn't have come as a surprise. In my pre-running life, I treated my body as if it were disposable. I had no connection to my body, so abusing it with cigarettes or food or alcohol didn't mean anything to me. Even when my body objected, like the times when I had to be rushed to the hospital because it seemed as if I was having a heart attack, I found a way to disassociate my behavior from the outcome.

I didn't become a new me when I started running. It turned out I was just as capable of doing damage to myself by overdoing something good as I had ever been at overdoing something bad.

Beyond the abject disrespect I had for my body, there was also the fact that I was totally ignorant of how my body functioned. I had never tried to live in my body. Hearing my heartbeat, listening to my own breathing, feeling the fatigue overcoming me were all new.

At first I thought it was a guy thing. I grew up in the John Wayne era of the man's man. As kids we would play war, or cowboys and Indians, and get shot all the time. There was an art to being injured— you had to grab the site of the injury and fall to the ground, only to bounce back up. No injury was enough to keep you down.

I took that same John Wayne mentality into my new running life. Knee pain? Grab the knee and keep going. Hip pain? Keep going. My mind-set was that I could run through anything. I had true grit. There was no pain too great, no risk too great, to stop me from running.

That is, until I found myself sitting on an examination table having a conversation with an orthopedic surgeon. My complaint was that my knee was killing me, and since I was preparing to run a marathon soon, I needed to get the situation addressed immediately.

I had ignored the 10 percent rule for increasing your weekly mileage. I wanted to get to where I was running close to 40 miles a week, and I had ramped up my mileage very quickly in order to get there.

Let's not forget that I was still running at barely a 10-minutes-per-mile pace, so 40 miles was close to eight hours of running per week.

The doc looked at my training log, which I had brought in to prove to him that I was capable of running the kind of mileage I was running and that the knee pain wasn't related to my stupidity. He noted the dramatic increase in mileage, and I explained that it was necessary in order for me to prepare for the marathon.

Sensing, I suppose, that I was stubborn and beyond reasoning with, he agreed to give me a shot of cortisone in my knee.

Now I knew the secret. You could overtrain, do stupid things, and hurt yourself—and there was a way to fix it.

Over the next couple of years I found myself sitting on that examination table a number of times. It might have been my knee, it might have been my hip;

it didn't matter. I knew the doc had the secret formula to make me feel better, and I wanted it.

Eventually he looked at me and said, "You're not 25 years old anymore. If you keep this up, you won't be able to run at all."

That was the last time I saw him. I figured if he didn't know how different my body was from every other body, then I wasn't going to continue to see him.

What I did next was become my own Dr. Frankenstein. I self-diagnosed and self-medicated in a futile attempt to erase the years of damage I had done to myself. I took massive dosages of anti-inflammatories, I wrapped and braced and strapped myself, all in order to keep running.

Before you assume that I am the only one who could possibly be this silly, just look around you at any race. You will see people with every kind of magic device, trying to avoid the truth about what they're doing to their bodies. For them, as it was for me, it isn't the running that creates the problems. It's ego. It's vanity. In my case, it was the irrational fear that if I quit running, even because I was injured, I'd never find the courage to start again.

So, as I said, every January it was the same thing. Every January I was starting over. Every January I worked out a training plan that called for me to be gentle on my body, that increased my mileage slowly, and that kept me healthy. And by every March I had given up on that plan.

A physical therapist explained to me once that she saw only two kinds of people in her practice: those who didn't use their bodies enough and those who used their bodies too much. As runners, we almost always fall into the category of those who use our bodies too much.

It turns out that to run for life, you have to learn to maintain your most important piece of equipment: yourself. It was a very difficult lesson for me to learn. For most of my life I had taken the opposite approach: I believed that if I *didn't* use my body, it would last forever. Considering that on the day of my very first run I owned nine motorcycles, two cars, a Volkswagen camper, a lawn tractor, and a gas-powered weed whacker, "exertion" was not in my vocabulary. Exertion was something I hired someone else to do. To exert myself was, well, unthinkable. I was an intellectual, after all. I did my work with my brain, not my body.

As a former motorcycle mechanic, though, I understood that for bikes to perform their best, they had to be maintained. I would spend hours and days adjusting and lubricating and polishing. I'd change the air filters on the vehicles so the engines would get clean air, all the while smoking a pack and a half of cigarettes a day, polluting my own lungs. I was a fanatic about the kinds of gas and oil that I used in the bikes, but I'd put any kind of junk inside myself.

But what I discovered, beginning with my very first run, was that unlike a piece of mechanical equipment, which wears out the more you use it, I actually got stronger the more I worked out. I was barely able to run (really it was more of a waddle) for a quarter of a mile that first day, but in just a few weeks I could cover an entire mile. It took me nearly 30 minutes, but I was able to do it.

I've learned that my body will do almost anything I ask of it as long as I give it time to adjust to new demands. I've been able to complete 45 marathons by gently coaxing my legs to go just a little farther every week. I've been able to run faster by pushing myself just a little harder every now and then.

> **To run for life, you have to learn to maintain your most important piece of equipment: yourself.**

The simple truth is that when it comes to our bodies, we really do have to use them or lose them. If we let them go to waste, we'll wake up one day and realize that even if we want to run, we can't. By not pushing ourselves we concede to an inevitable decline, a loss of mobility, a future in which we become prisoners in our own bodies.

I've learned that the way to make your body last is to use it. The way to make sure all the internal parts are working is by moving all the external parts. And most important, whether your goal is to run 1 mile, to complete your first 5K, or to qualify for the Boston Marathon, understand that your body is a marvelous machine and you are your own mechanic.

Over the years I've gotten better at recognizing the early signs of an overuse injury—the quiet ache, the nagging tightness that precedes a full-blown outbreak—but it's been hard to accept that in order to be a runner, you have to *not* run sometimes. I've never really been able to shake loose my fear that if I quit running, even if it's for all the right reasons, I'll never be able to come back.

That fear is based on my belief that it's easier to start from scratch than it is to start again. When I started from scratch, I had no idea what to expect. In my joyous naïveté I just did what I needed to do. But when you're starting over, your body and your brain are at odds. That belief has been confirmed by thousands of e-mails from injured runners, former runners, and wannabe runners. When you start with nothing, you have nothing to lose.

When you're coming back from an injury or an extended layoff, your mind remembers what it was like when you were in your prime. Your mind remembers what it felt like to be able to run for as long as you wanted, or as fast as you wanted.

Your mind remembers the moments of exhilaration—picking up the pace at the end of a race or hitting some new mileage number. Your mind remembers, but your body doesn't.

Our bodies have very bad short-term memories. Anyone who has ever run a marathon one Sunday and then struggled to get through a 3-mile run the next weekend knows what I'm talking about. Our bodies forget everything they've learned almost immediately. At least it seems that way.

I think I kept running through the pain and the injuries because I was afraid that the will I had to begin the first time wouldn't be there when I needed to begin again.

What I didn't recognize was that, through running, I had undergone a fundamental change in who I was. My fear of not being able to come back didn't take into account that, injured or not, I was a runner.

It's difficult to accept, but the truth is that sometimes you are a better runner when you choose not to run for a while.

At this stage of my life it's nearly impossible for me to imagine not being a runner. I don't know what I'd do if I couldn't run or walk. I would stop being who I am if I had to give up the activity that *makes* me who I am.

I am learning to accept that taking time away from running in order to keep running is something I have to do. If I want to be able to run forever, I may not be able to run today.

I don't want to have to face another January injured. I don't want to be the guy who looks like he just escaped from a medical-supply store.

One of the greatest gifts I've received from running has also been one of the most difficult truths to accept: I've had to learn that I am human.

My body is not unique or special. I am certainly not gifted. My body functions in exactly the same way that every other body functions. If I am kind to my body, it works well. If I abuse my body, it will eventually shut down.

The extension of that truth is that the same rules that apply to my body apply to the rest of me. I am human not just in body but in mind and spirit.

I spent the early part of my life not just abusing my body with smoking and drinking and overeating but abusing my spirit as well. When my body became loaded down with weight, it buried my spirit.

Running has taught me, and continues to teach me, that there is joy in accepting the fact that I am fully human. I am susceptible to all the trials and tribulations that we all have to face. I cannot hide from them. I cannot escape from them. I have to meet them head-on. And maybe that is *true* true grit.

I have not faced my final injury. I have not confronted my last comeback. I know that another time will come when I will have to start over from scratch.

The difference is that these days I face that challenge with the knowledge that not only did I have the courage to start, but I have the courage to start again and again.

FIFTEEN

WHEN LESS IS MORE

I'm not crazy about getting older. I'm in my 60s now, which, for someone who never thought he'd make it past 30, seems like quite an accomplishment. In fact, in the words of the late baseball great Mickey Mantle, if I'd known I was going to live this long, I would have taken better care of myself.

But getting older isn't all bad. With each passing year, I find that I worry less about what other people think and more about how I feel. Don't get me wrong—I love the idea of making people happy. Now, though, I recognize that I can't please everyone all of the time, so I'm able to spend more time finding ways of sustaining my own happiness.

When I was younger I was sure that more was better. I wanted more money, more house, more job, more responsibilities, more everything. I judged myself against everyone else by whether or not I had more than they did.

As a runner I took the same approach. If 3 miles was good, 4 was better. If one marathon a year was good, six a year were better. I didn't understand that I could find satisfaction in quality because I only understood quantity.

The idea that more is always better than less is an especially pernicious myth when it comes to a life of activity. It can become a disastrous belief as you age as a runner.

I've got a good friend in his late 50s who is what I define as a "nylon shorts" runner. He's old school. He's been running for most of his life, and he's never met a hard workout that he didn't like. The typical day for him is to pound out a 7-or-more-mile run. It doesn't matter what he's training for; he just goes out and runs hard.

When he was younger this approach worked pretty well for him. He could run hard all the time, then sign up for a race and expect a strong performance from himself. It didn't matter if it was a local 5K or a major-league marathon. His philosophy was the same: Train hard. Race hard.

Recently he's started to complain that he can't keep up with the young guys anymore. I look at him sternly and ask why he thinks he should be able to keep up. His response is that he's doing what he's always done, so the results should be the same. He's lost sight of the truth that your running self can't be separated from the rest of yourself. We age. We grow. We change.

> *As I've gotten older, I've had to learn how to negotiate with my body.*

There was a time in the history of running when everyone worshiped at the altar of mileage. The only thing that mattered was that number in your log at the end of the week. The higher the number, the better the week.

Professional marathoners in those days were running weeks of over 150 miles. Think that through for a minute: over 150 miles a week. And they weren't just doing it for one week; they were doing it for months at a time.

The theory was simple: The more you run, the better you get at running. That sounds good on the surface, but it turns out to be false. As an old education professor once told me about classroom instruction, "Kids learn what they do and damn little else." Sure, you'll learn how to run if you run a lot, but you'll only learn how to keep running the way you're running.

Many of us begin our running lives believing that old myth. I did. I believed that in order for me to be a runner, I had to run as much as possible, and the more I ran, the better runner I would be.

As I explained in Chapter 14, that wasn't the case. More often than not, by running more I ended up having to run less—or in some cases ended up not being able to run at all.

We reach a point as runners where less really is more. My experience has been that it comes at major age thresholds and at watershed years in our running lives.

Since I didn't start running until I was over the age of 40, I can't speak from personal experience about what it's like to run before you turn 40 and then to cross that threshold. I can tell you, though, what I've seen and heard from thousands of runners who have.

Somewhere around age 40 your body's ability to restore and renew itself begins to slip. It isn't dramatic at first. You may notice that you don't have quite as much energy as you used to the day after a hard work-out. You may notice that it just isn't as much fun to do back-to-back long days.

When you're under the age of 40, it takes about 24 hours for your body to recover from a hard work-out. That translates into being able to run just about every day if you want to.

After age 40 it takes close to 48 hours for your body to fully recover. What that means is that by running too much, too hard, too far, too often, you may actually get worse instead of better.

This doesn't mean that you can't run every day, but it does mean that you have to consider what you're trying to accomplish with every run. Each one can't be a work of art, so some will have to be just runs.

After age 50 the cumulative effects of having been on the planet for half a century really begin to appear. Gravity can't be denied, and parts of your body that were once well north of your center of gravity start to make their way down.

After 50 your joints, tendons, and all the connective tissue start to show signs of wear. It's not that you're ready for the rocking chair, but you do begin to notice that it's a little harder to do what you've always done.

By 60 everything begins to change. It isn't just your body; your mind, your soul, your spirit, and even your will begin to concede the truth of how many years have passed since you arrived on the planet. At 60 plus, I find that I am simultaneously more and less connected to everything around me.

I am more connected because I know how fleeting those connections can be. I am less connected for the same reason. Nothing lasts forever.

I've found that the best way to accommodate these changes is by accepting them as natural and necessary. Fighting them won't work.

When I start to make a training schedule for myself now, I begin with the rest days. I know I will need to build in rest days and that if I don't put them in up front, they will somehow get left out.

When I'm training now, I try to find the most efficient way to achieve my goals. I try to find the least risky ways of building mileage. I make sure there is always an alternative to doing one harder workout.

I'm also trying to find activities to complement my running that do not impose the same kind of pounding on my body. I walk more, not because I have to but because I want to. I haven't conceded anything; I just feel that I've discovered a better way to stay active. I've returned to bicycling as both a recreational activity and a cross-training sport. I've even found that I can take a day completely off and not feel that it's a waste of time.

What I've noticed is that the less I can run, the more I appreciate the times that I do run. If it's true that absence makes the heart grow fonder, then not running has made me much fonder of running.

If you find yourself at a point in your running life where the fun just doesn't seem to be there anymore, it may be time to consider whether you need to run less in order to enjoy it more. I can tell you for sure that if you have lost the joy in your running, it won't be long before you will lose the will to run.

I started running because I knew that at some level something was missing in my life. I didn't know what it was exactly, but I can tell you this: I took to running with the enthusiasm and eagerness of an animal released from a cage. The more I ran, the more I could run, and the more I wanted to run. There was no horizon that I couldn't run to. Even though I ran slowly, I ran free. I ran uninhibited.

That sense of release from the bondage of my sedentary body was overwhelming. I couldn't get enough of it. There weren't enough hours in the day to run and to think about running. I would spend hours working out elaborate training schedules.

In the early years of my running career I was transported on the wave of constant improvement. It seemed as if every race brought a new best time, every training session brought a new sense of enlightenment about myself, and every time I laced up my shoes was an opportunity to discover a new secret about myself.

I've written before that through those early years, my running shoes felt like erasers, rubbing away the physical, emotional, and spiritual graffiti of my life. The changes on my inside were just as obvious as the changes on my outside.

But like any relationship, my relationship with running was bound to move past those heady early days when everything seemed perfect to the stark reality that not every run would be a mind-blowing experience. I progressed to a place in my relationship with running where I began to seek a balance between the runner I was and the runner I wanted to be.

As I've gotten older, I've had to learn how to negotiate with my body. I've had to learn how to compromise with the parts that won't automatically do what I want them to do.

In my early days of running, I would very often do that dance with the devil where I spent all my time on the edge of my ability. I tried to walk a tightrope between improvement and injury. Now, as a seasoned runner, I have come to appreciate the miracle that I am a runner at all. I am far less likely to risk not being able to run forever because I think I must run today.

I don't need the constant reinforcement from running that I needed in those early years. Then, I was looking to running as the answer to everything that was wrong with me. I believed that by running I would eventually run away from all my problems. It wasn't true. Running never solved any of my problems, but it did provide me with a forum in which I could consider how to solve them. Running provided a structure and a model upon which I could consider problems in my life. Running taught me that very often what I thought was one giant problem, like running a marathon, was actually a series of smaller problems that could be solved in sequence.

> *I know that every step is a step in the right direction, taking me closer to who I want to be.*

As my relationship with running deepened, I found that I had much more confidence in my ability to remain a runner. That may sound strange when you consider that over the years my pace has slowed and my mileage has dropped, but the truth is that I am more sure of myself as a runner now than I have ever been.

In the early days of my running, I believed that I wasn't a real runner if someone else said I wasn't. I didn't run at the right pace or over the right distance. I would allow other people to steal my vision of myself as a runner when it didn't match their vision.

What I finally understand is that the only person who can tell me whether or not I'm a runner is me. I finally recognize that running more doesn't make me more of a runner; it just means I'm running more. Running faster doesn't make me more of a runner; it just means I'm running faster.

After nearly 20 years of running, it has finally sunk in that in order to be a runner, all I really have to do is run. Just run! What a liberating thought.

Once I got it into my head that by running I was— by definition—a runner, everything about running got better. All the fears, the pressure, and the worries went away. What a wonder that here, in the winter running season of my life, the joy I felt the very first time I ran is back. It's back because I know that every step is a step in the right direction, taking me closer to who I want to be—which is, after all, the gift that running has always given me.

SIXTEEN

ONE DAY AT A TIME

Members of 12-step programs such as Alcoholics Anonymous live by the adage "one day at a time." I never really understood what that meant. After all, how can you live any other way than one day at a time? But at some point, probably while out on a run, I realized that I was living about 49 percent of my life in the past, about 49 percent in the future, and only about 2 percent in the present.

That was certainly true about my running life. I was usually so consumed with what I had been running and what I was going to run that I didn't have the time or energy to really be in the run I was on.

You'll notice this phenomenon if you find yourself around runners who are preparing for some major future race. The race they're in is never the race that matters. The race they're in is only a tune-up for some race that is still to come.

Runners of this kind are often unhappy with the race they've run. I've seen them cross the finish line ranting and shouting because they missed their personal-best time by three seconds. They will sulk back to their cars and, I imagine, berate themselves all the way home.

We need to be careful not to look so far ahead that we miss what's right at our feet.

What I find sad about this absence of grace at the finish line is that these people are ignoring one of life's basic tenets: We don't know what tomorrow will bring. We don't know when, or if, we'll ever be given the opportunity to see another finish line.

However, I can't say I don't understand it. Make no mistake, I was the same way for a long time. Once I started running, once running had become a part of my identity, I began to take the enormous gift of my ability to run for granted. I assumed that the experiences I was having would go on forever. I couldn't imagine a time when what I was feeling would end.

I got it into my head that I was somehow entitled to the joy of running because I was willing to put in the time to train. It was as if I had struck a bargain with the universe that in exchange for my having the discipline and desire to be a runner, the powers that be would grant me unlimited opportunities to run. It's not the case.

Too often, it seems to me, we miss the most important reasons to run because we're so busy running. We get so caught up in the days and weeks and miles of a training plan that we run right past experiences that would make all the training worthwhile. The goal of any training plan may be absolutely worthwhile—reaching a new distance, achieving a faster time, raising money for a cause—but we need to be careful not to look so far ahead that we miss what's right at our feet.

I should have learned the lesson of being in the moment from my life as a musician. I spent years practicing and performing. I spent years playing great music with great musicians. Yet, sadly, I didn't enjoy very much of it.

Like those runners griping at the finish line, I would finish a concert and be able to think about nothing but my own performance. I might have been able to experience a life-changing moment of pure musical bliss if I had only been able to forget about myself for an instant.

I see this in races when one runner finishes disgruntled and dissatisfied right next to someone else who is weeping with joy. I wonder how in the world they could not share the same experience. But I already know the answer.

The answer is that it's very difficult for any of us to live in the moment, let alone *run* in the moment. It is difficult to set aside everything that has happened and that might happen in order to be present for what is happening right now.

I had an experience while motorcycling that made the point of living in the moment very clear. The lesson was clear, but I wasn't quite ready to learn it.

I had been on a monthong motorcycle trip and had traveled from Annapolis to Sacramento on U.S. Route 50. I had then ridden down the coast of California and back up the center of California, then through Nevada, Idaho, Montana, and Wyoming. On this particular day I was outside Pierre, South Dakota.

It had been a long day near the end of a long trip. I had lingered too long in the Black Hills National Forest. It was late. It was dark. And I was tired.

I was riding much too fast for the two-lane highway that I was on, but nothing in me was saying, "Slow down." I could see only to the edge of the area illuminated by my headlight, no farther. The light was punching a narrow hole in the darkness, and all I could do was ride through it.

It occurred to me even as I was riding that nothing outside that narrow beam of light mattered to me.

I didn't know what was to the left or to the right of me, and I didn't care. If it didn't come into the light, it wasn't important.

I could see the pavement passing underneath me. I knew that once my wheels had covered that ground I would never see it again. What was ahead of me was unknown. What was behind me was of no consequence.

At that speed I had no choice but to be in the moment, focused on the outer edge of my headlight. I rode that way for hours, transfixed by a single spot in front of me, which contained my entire world even as the world around me changed constantly.

Some might call that a Zen-like experience. I don't know enough about Zen to know whether that is true. All I know is that on that night the only way I could stay alive was to live inside the light.

What I want most for myself as a runner, and for those whom I'm fortunate enough to encounter or influence as runners, is to learn to run inside our own light, to experience the transformation that occurs when we are no longer what we were and not yet what we will be. We are only what we are.

I've been lucky because I have been aware enough at times to know that I was living inside my own light. And I have been blessed by times when I have been able to share someone else's light.

> *We can all find the right way forward if we're willing to take the risk of moving off the spot we're on.*

There was a morning run on a trail outside Boston when our group arrived at a large field of grass covered in dew. We all just stopped and stood looking at this magnificently ordinary field of grass that had, for one instant, made us all more attuned to where we were.

There was an encounter with a middle-aged man at mile 15 of the Chicago Marathon who broke down in tears because no one had ever cheered for him before.

There was the friend who completed a marathon just weeks after losing a breast to cancer, who collapsed into my arms and cried for the first time since her diagnosis.

Like so many others, I took my first running steps because I thought it would help me lose weight. I also thought it would give me a healthier heart. That was what I wanted from running. I wanted it to live up to the promises I'd heard.

I have come to realize that running makes no promises to me. It doesn't promise to make me thinner or smarter. It doesn't promise to make me live longer. Being a runner doesn't entitle me to anything other than that act of running. And that's enough.

My running now, 19 years after I took my first step, is a celebration. I've been through the times of wanting to get faster or go farther. I've conceded that my fastest days—if not my best days—as a runner are behind me. And I acknowledge that I have to find a way to run that brings significance to me, and only me.

Robert A. Johnson wrote a wonderful little book titled *He*. It is an interpretation of the legend of the Holy Grail as experienced by Parsifal. I admit that the Monty Python version is funnier, but Johnson's book is well worth reading.

After years of searching for his own truth and happiness, Parsifal returns to the Grail castle. He is required to answer just one question: Whom does the Grail serve? The answer is that the Grail serves the Grail king.

I'm not sure I understand every philosophical nuance of that answer. However, what I took from it was this: The things that are serve the things that they are. Not to get too metaphysical about it, but I think that means that the earth is here not to serve us but to serve itself. Trees and flowers may be beautiful to observe, but they were just as beautiful before we got here and would serve just as important a role if we had never seen them.

In the same way, I used to believe that running existed to serve me, almost as if I were the one who first discovered running and was entitled to all the gifts and pleasures it had to offer.

I took running to be the replacement for the other pleasures in my life that I had given up. If I couldn't find pleasure in eating because I was living a healthier lifestyle, then running would have to make up the difference. If I were going to give up the pleasure of smoking, then running would have to give me the same kind of euphoria.

I was willing to do the work. I was willing to put in the miles, to run in the rain or in the heat, but I demanded that running return the favor. I demanded that running serve me and serve me well.

What I didn't know was what Parsifal didn't know. Running wasn't ever going to serve me. Running would be everything that it is and ever has been even if I had never taken a running step.

I also tried to make running a multipurpose activity. At first, like so many others, I used running simply as a way to burn calories so I could eat more of what I wanted and still lose weight. Of course that never works because you can consume calories so much more quickly than you can burn them.

Later I used running to feel better about myself. As I lost weight, got more active, and started running and racing more often, I looked to running to bring me the peace of mind and contentedness that was missing in my life. That doesn't work either because eventually you have to stop running and go back to living your life.

Still later I used running to prop up my ego and my sense of self. I was no longer content to define myself as just a runner; I had to be a *long-distance* runner. As with any addiction, I gradually needed more and more running to get the same feeling. When one marathon a year no longer made me feel like a runner, I ran more.

I frequently see people who are running marathons every month or every week, and I know what's going on. They are looking for that bigger and bigger fix.

In the end I believe that the best reason to run is simply because you can.

Each day that I get to run is a gift, not an entitlement. Each day that I get to spend as a member of the running community is a day I can treasure.

If it is true that we can—and should—learn to live one day at a time, then I think it is also true that we can—and should—learn to run one day at a time. Each time we put on our shoes we should be present for whatever that run gives us.

We can forget about what we did yesterday and not worry about what we're going to do tomorrow. We can live our running life literally one step at a time.

I am a runner. I am an athlete. I am an accidental athlete. I came to this life as an athlete not because I wanted to so much as because I didn't know what else to do. I was lost, and the only way out was with my own two feet.

We can all find that path to ourselves with our own two feet. We can all find the right way forward if we're willing to take the risk of moving off the spot we're on.

It is easier than most people think it is to be an athlete. It is also much more difficult. Being an athlete means taking risks, reaching for something beyond your grasp, and accepting failure as an integral part of success.

It's a little like having a third emotional eye. We cannot only see who we've been and who we want to be; we can see with absolute clarity who we are right now.

Being an athlete doesn't mean that you are *athletic*. Being an athlete means that you are committed to encountering the world around you with the courage and conviction of an athlete.

If you have that courage to think and live and feel like an athlete, then you will find, as I have, that you have more strength of will and body than you ever dreamed possible.

All it takes to begin is a single step.

RUNNING INTO MYSELF

When it gets really, really quiet in my head—
which isn't often—I wonder what and who
I would have been if I hadn't become a runner.
I wonder what my life would look like now, 20 years
after I started running, if I had done what I had
always done before: quit.

I was a 21-day enthusiast for most of my life.
Whenever I wanted to do, or to be, anything, I could
find the enthusiasm to do it for only about 21 days.
What's remarkable, looking back, is how wide-ranging
my interests were and how wholly unabated by ratio-
nal thought my ambitions were.

My basement and garage are littered with the
equipment of my abandoned dreams. There is the
tennis racket from when I was convinced that I could

be the next Wimbledon champion. Or at least I thought I could learn how to play a decent game.

I couldn't—not in 21 days anyway. My tennis playing consisted mostly of chasing balls around the court, swinging and missing, or connecting and sending them over the fence like home-run balls. So I quit.

I wanted to be good at waterskiing. Those 21 days were spread out over a couple of summers, but the result was the same. I came. I tried. I failed.

It turns out that one of the primary skills you need to be good at waterskiing is a sense of when to let go of the rope. I did not possess that skill. My approach was to cling with a death grip to the rope long after I had fallen face-first into the water. This approach, as you can imagine, resulted in my nearly drowning—not just once, mind you. Over and over again.

I did finally manage to get up on the skis. Well, I managed to get out of the water and into some kind of bent-knee stance that made me look like a marionette whose strings had broken. I would be pulled behind the boat until my arms got tired, and then, without letting go of the rope, I would fall into the water.

It never got much better than that. So I quit.

I thought maybe I could learn to kayak. I like the water, and the idea of paddling peacefully down a slow-moving river sounded nice. So I signed up for a paddling class.

It was all going fine until we got the kayaks into the water. I remember the instructor telling us to sit very still in the kayaks until we got a sense of what it felt like to stay balanced. At least, I think that was what he said, but I'm not sure because as he was saying it I was turning over, facedown, in the Chicago River, strapped into the kayak with the skirt attached.

Despite sheer panic, I was somehow able to release the skirt and get back to the surface. On the bright side, it gave the instructor the opportunity to teach rescue technique to the rest of the class.

Then there was the time I decided I wanted to learn to fish, thinking it would be a great father-son bonding experience. I bought the equipment, rented a boat, got a container of night crawlers, and—with my son in the boat—rowed out to the middle of the small lake, where we first lost the anchor and then dropped one of the oars into the water, watched it float away, and spent the next hour trying to figure out how to paddle over to it.

This is not a complete list of my failed attempts to be more active and more of an athlete. But I think you get the point. My desire to be athletic far exceeded my abilities.

What made running so magical for me was that almost from the first step I *got it*. I understood what it was to run, what it was to be a runner, and what it was to be alone with myself. I wasn't any good at it; that was obvious. But I understood what I was trying to do.

Every run—even if it was only lots of walking with an occasional jog at first—opened some window into my mind or soul. Every step seemed to have the potential to unlock some mystery buried inside me.

When I ran from my childhood home, for example, down the streets and sidewalks that I played on during my elementary school years, I could hear the voices, see the faces, and feel the feelings from those days. I could feel the presence of my childhood friends.

I felt the shame from those days, the embarrassment at who I was, the disappointment of my repeated failures to be "as good" as everyone else. I ran through that neighborhood with a heavy heart.

When I got to the schoolyard, to the same piece of asphalt where I had played, to the same basketball hoops and baseball fields, it was as if I was releasing all of those feelings. I was there again, but this time I was there as a runner. Not a very good runner, but a runner nonetheless.

That sense of release from the bondage of my past, of clearing away the memories that served no purpose but to keep me chained to an image of myself that was no longer true, happened to me over and over again in the early years. It was as if I were undoing all the emotional knots—and "nots"—that were holding me back.

The hardest transition for many of us who are adult-onset athletes is to go from viewing ourselves as athletic failures to accepting that we are finally, truly, athletes.

> *As a runner I have had to reach deeply into myself, and when I have, I've discovered a mighty reserve of strength.*

It doesn't seem to matter how successful we have been at other things or how much we've achieved in another arena; if we don't heal the wounds of our past failures, athletic and otherwise, none of it matters. Or at least it didn't to me.

I've seen a running t-shirt that says, "Cheaper Than Therapy." There's a lot of truth in that. I tried therapy but found that the answers I was searching for were easier to find on a run.

As I continued to run, as my running became more and more central to my life, I noticed a subtle but significant change in my attitude toward myself. The more I ran, the more running revealed to me who I was; the more I became aware of the truth about myself, the less inclined I was to let anyone else define me.

Now that running is integral to my life, now that I am running not because I have to but simply because

I can, the insights into my essential self are perhaps less dramatic but no less profound.

I know I am stronger than I ever imagined I could be. Not stronger so much in a physical sense as in the sense that I feel capable of facing any of life's challenges. Bring them on! As a runner I have had to reach deeply into myself, and when I have, I've discovered a mighty reserve of strength.

I face the challenges—of growing older, of changing relationships, of the good and bad of being alive—in the same way that I face the challenges of running. I now know that, in running and in life, there will be good patches and bad and that neither lasts forever. And I've learned that having a good plan is fine as long as I accept that nothing ever goes according to plan.

In the final analysis, running has taught me how to live. I have learned, with my own two feet, the meaning of triumph and failure, and the fleeting nature of both.

I have learned, through running, that the truth of any given moment is the only truth I can know for sure.

And the truth I know at this moment is that I am a runner.

Waddle on, friends.

ACKNOWLEDGMENTS

In preparing to write the acknowledgments for this book, I went back and read the acknowledgments in my first book, *The Courage to Start* (New York: Fireside, 1999). Two things struck me: one, how many of the people whom I needed to thank back then are still in my life, and two, how many aren't.

It's important to recognize Marlene Cimons, Amby Burfoot, and Sue Flaster. None of them may ever see this acknowledgment, yet without them this book would never have been written.

I also acknowledged my family. In the intervening years I have lost some of those who were important to me, but I have gained three wonderful grandchildren who remind me that there is joy to be found in even the most mundane activities and that the excitement that follows self-discovery begins at a very early age.

There are new people in my life whose influence cannot be overstated. They have names like Paul, and Pete, and Jon, and Dan. Simple names. Simple people, yet without their daily guidance and good counsel, I might not have gotten to this place.

My professional world has changed from writing in isolation to being accessible 24 hours a day by e-mail and the social media. I encounter thousands of runners and walkers every year, and each of them teaches me something. Their lives and their experiences, as well as my own, live on the pages of this book.

My wife, coach, coauthor, teammate, cheerleader, and critic, Jenny Hadfield, opened my world just by being who she is. Her courage and curiosity are contagious. My life is richer, fuller, and more satisfying with her in it than it has ever been.

I am grateful to all of them, each in their own way, for helping me find myself.

Finally, special thanks to Casey Blaine and Connie Oehring at VeloPress for making my words come to life.

ABOUT THE AUTHOR

He's been called the Pied Piper of the second running boom. Since his column, "The Penguin Chronicles," started in *Runner's World* magazine in 1996, John "The Penguin" Bingham has become one of the running community's most popular and recognized personalities. Now that he is a feature columnist for *Competitor* magazine and a weekly blogger on Competitor.com, his popularity continues to grow.

Bingham is a national spokesperson for the Leukemia and Lymphoma Society's Team in Training and principal announcer at the Competitor Group's Rock 'n' Roll Marathon series. He is in constant demand as a clinician and has been a featured speaker at the Boston, Chicago, New York City, London, Nike Women's, Marine Corps, Honolulu, and Portland marathons and at the Rock 'n' Roll series events in Phoenix, Dallas, New Orleans, Nashville, San Diego, Seattle, Chicago, Philadelphia, Los Angeles, San Antonio, and Las Vegas.

His first book, *The Courage to Start: A Guide to Running for Your Life*, has been among the top 10 running books since its publication. His second book, *No Need for Speed: A Beginner's Guide to the Joy of Running*, became the manifesto for the second running boom. His best-selling training books, *Marathoning for Mortals: A Regular Person's Guide to the Joy of Running or Walking a Full or Half Marathon* and *Running for Mortals: A Commonsense Plan for Changing Your Life with Running*, were coauthored with his wife, Coach Jenny Hadfield.

The *New York Times* recently identified Bingham as the father of the slow running movement that has brought the joy of activity to an entire new generation of runners and walkers.

For more information on John "The Penguin" Bingham, go to http://accidentalathlete.com.